He's Been a Cloud over Me All My Life with Love, Love, and More Love

By Jehovah through the Heart, Mind, and Left-hand of

KEVIN MOSS

First Edition

NEWMAN SPRINGS PUBLISHING
320 Broad Street
Red Bank, NJ 07701

First originally published by Newman Springs Publishing 2023

All the scriptures written in *He's Been a Cloud Over Me All My Life With Love, Love and More Love* do come from the King James Version Bible.

ISBN 978-1-63881-758-1 (Paperback)
ISBN 978-1-63881-759-8 (Digital)

Printed in the United States of America

I dedicate this to the poor and the needy
in the name of Jesus Christ.

Contents

He's Been a Cloud over Me All My Life Part 1 11
With Love, Love, and More Love! 33
Beautiful, Unique, and True 34
A Man! 36
Thou Shall Not Kill! 38
God Doesn't Like Ugly! 40
With His and My Strength I'll Make It 42
It's Not about Money, but All about Love 44
Paper and Fire Just Don't Mix 46
It's God's Way or the Highway 47
God's Word Will Always Stand! 48
My Feet Stand on His 50
I Chose You 52
I Know It Was the Blood 54
Pick up Your Cross and Follow Me 55
The Ten Commandments 57
Know I'm at the Door 59
You Can Play Games or You Can Gain Life 61
Being on the Winning Team 63
You've Seen the Lord 65
Up, Up, Up 67
He Vibrates In My Heart And Circles In My Mind! 69
Only the Love of Father Can Fill the Hole Left by Mother! 71
Who Said a Male Can't Cry? 73
Looks Fake but It's Real! 75
But Love Is! 77
The Moon, the Stars, and You! 78
Two Wrongs Doesn't Make a Right! 80

Beginning to End, End to Beginning 82
You Can't Judge a Book by the Cover! 84
Their Truly One, One, One! 86
Eternally Burn! 88
Your Word Is Your Bind 90
Another Link in God's Chain 91
Pastor Month 93
A Strong Foundation 95
We All Come Together, Truly We Are One 97
What Happened to Respect? 99
There's Only One Judge 100
I Shall Judge All! 102
I Am That I Am 104
A Blind Leads Another into a Deep, Deep Hole 106
The Trumpet Shall Be Blown 107
Eternal 109
All Shall Bow to Me 111
Just Another Part of Life 112
The Table Does Turn 114
May We Be Lifted Up 116
Priority and Order 118
A Butterfly Flew in My Window 120
My Rabbit, Bear, and Cat 121
Faith, Truth, and Love 123
I Wish, I Wish, I Wish! 125
We Too Are One 127
Hide-and-Seek! 129
Looks like I Have Nothing but I Have It All 132
Filled and Covered 134
Now You're Truly One 136
Time's Running Out 138
You Are What You Eat 140
Testimony, Praise, and More Praise 141
There's Two Sides to Every Story 143
True Is the Heart 145
Nothing Else but Love! 146

The Truth, the Truth, the Truth Is Nothing but the Truth! 148
Do You Think You Can? 150
Our World Tomorrow 152
Gone but Not Forgotten 153
Wake up, Everyone, for You Most Be Sleeping 154
We Have Another Chance 156
Are You Ready? 158
Walking the Golden Sidewalk 160
Wrong, Wrong, Wrong, Is Nothing Else but Wrong 162
Over and Over Again 164
He That Sinnith Not Cast the First Stone 165
Where Are We Now? 166
Who Said We Can't or Won't When We Already Are? 168
May I Kiss His Every Toe 169
The Comforter 170
Christ, Head of the Temple and King of God's Army 172
Let Jesus Get You Over, Across, and Through 174
Eight-Ball Corner Pocket 175
These Perilous, Perilous Days 177
It's God's Word That Stands 179
The Door of Doors 181
A Little Water on My Tongue 183
In Six Days 184
Another Beautiful Day 186
A Mother's Love 187
How Can One Not Love, Love? 189
Who Gave the Most 191
Thank You, Thank You, Thank You 193
Ho, Ho, Ho 195
"The Whole Armor of God" 197
Ephesians 6:14–18 197
Cast Him under Your Feet 199
No Matter How Many Times You Fall 201
Your Eyes Are Open, But You Still Not See 202
Three Different Flavors with One Delicious Topping 204
He's So, So Real, and It's Oh So True 206

We All Come Together, for Truly We Are One 207
How Can One Go a Day without God? 209
We're Truly, Truly Blessed 210
Who Cast Down Who? 212
Walking on Water 214
He That's First Will Be Last and He on the
Top Will Be on the Bottom 216
Every Stone Shall Fall 217
Don't False Teach My Children 219
He's Always There 221
All Must Forgive All 223
Time Goes On 225
A Beautiful Flower 227
Yield, Stop, and Go! 229
May We Learn to Blow Out Angels of Love 230
The Love of Jesus Christ Day and Night 232
Happiness, Peace, and Joy Is God the Greatest 233
The New Heaven Earth 235
The Meaning of Happiness, Peace, and Joy 237
Such a Lovely Friend 239
Just One 241
With Love May We Kiss Again, Again, and Again 243
We Must, We Must, We Must! 245
My Word Shall Always Stand 246
I Will to Do His Will 248
Through Love and Faith We Sail 250
Two but One 252
Did You Thank the Lord? 254
Thanks for Another Day 255
The Heart and the Mind 257
Lost but Found 258
The True Color of Love! 260
A Manipulator 262
First, Not Last 264
Nothing's Free and Lasts Forever but God's Love 266
Forgive We All 268

Jehovah, Yes, God Is Love, Love, and More Love........................269
Get Thy Hence 271
The Word Was God 273
Let Him In........................275
My Lord, My Lord, My God, Truly Do I Thank You 277
Erick, Derek, and Damon 279
We Must Find a Way!........................281
Grace, Grace, Grace 282
Love, Peace, and Soul with Happiness, Peace, and Joy........................284
H2O 286
You Can Have More Than One........................288
One Wonderful Two That Are Truly Only One........................290
God's Good........................291
Turn the Other Cheek........................292
The Bright Shining Light 294
There's Only One I Praise and Bow Down To! 296
First Is Last and Top Is Bottom........................298
Chaos or Love, Who's Your Choice? 300
You Can't Escape the Eclipse 302
Love and Need Are Two Different Things 304
Let God Put Us Back Together........................306
He's Been A Cloud Over Me All My Life Part 2 308
A Stubborn People 319
The Perilous Times Of The Last Days 320
The Greatest, The Greatest, The Greatest,
God's Just The Greatest! 321

He's Been a Cloud over Me All My Life Part 1

You know, sometimes our lives can seem so dark that at times we even become scared of ourselves. Sounds kind of crazy, right? Well, it shouldn't, for sometimes some of us really end up feeling just that way, but we don't have too, okay? And why's that, I guess you say? Well, that's because through Jehovah, yes, God, we are able to get back what we all had lost, yes, eternal Life. And that's through Jesus Christ, yes, Jesus Christ, God's first love being sent out to us all, yes, to us all that do believe that Jesus Christ is the first Son of God and that He willingly gave His life for all when He willingly died on the cross and, by Him willingly dying on the cross, giving His, He also became the way for us to get back ours. Now believing this with all your heart, mind, body, and soul is something you must do to one day be able to truly enter the true kingdom of God, which then shall be called the New Heaven Earth. Yes, it's here that we shall enter through the Golden Gates and be rewarded with the crown of glory and eternal life. But first we must give God all praise and glory for truly it's His, because it was He who loved we the world so much that for us, He gave the life of His only begotten Son, Jesus Christ, the saving Messiah. And He, the Son, so loved His Father and we His world that He did willingly give His life, and once again by willingly giving His, He also became the way for us to get back ours. And may we all knowingly hold this in our heart with faith! Know ye not that the only way to the Father is through He, Jesus Christ, the first Son? And the Son had the same love for the Father and we, His world, as the Father had for we, the world, when He gave the life of His only begotten Son by sending Him down to His earth below from His heaven high above just to die for our sins; yes, Jesus Christ surely died for we the world with love, love, and more love. Also may we all the world know and believe that they're truly One, One, One. Now I want to share another story with you pertaining to me, myself, and God's love and also His Word, and this, I'm sure, will show you how God's love and Word is just as strong now as it was way back then. Yes, way back then when He did truly say, to we the world, "Never will I leave you and never will I forsake you." Yes, truly this He did say to we all the world. Now I, Kevin Moss, was born and raised in the city of Wilmington of the state of Delaware. Now at 8 years old, I went to an elementary school by the name of Lore. And across the street from the school stood a park, and at the front of the park was a baseball diamond, and for some reason, which I now believe was spiritual, whenever I would look out the classroom window over at this park, I would see a big red dragon that stood at the back of the park; and whenever I would see this dragon, believe me, I wouldn't see or hear anything else. Now at this time we were between the years of 1968 and 1969, and if I'm not mistaken, at that time children as myself who was still a child of the time were raised a lot different back then than they are today, would not you say? And I believe a good reason for that is, back then it seemed parents had a lot more patience for their children than they do today, and let's not forget, back then children were very well disciplined and were taught respect from the start and most children loved and respected most elders and most their elders loved and respected them too. For instance, back when I was a child growing up, if one of your elders would happen to see you doing something one day that they and you also know you weren't supposed to be doing, most of them would pop you upside your head or smack you on your bottom. Then they would usually yank you up and take you home to your mother and tell her just what they saw you doing. And most of our mother's response or reaction would usually be something like "He did what?" And she'd then take you in the house and, with a belt or extension cord, would wear your legs and buttocks out so bad that whatever you had been caught doing to get the spanking in the first place, I bet you didn't do it anymore or at least no time soon, and that's for sure. Now God tells us in the book of Proverbs in the Bible, which was always my favorite book, but as I was saying, in the book of Proverbs 23:13–14, through King Solomon God says, "Withhold not correction from the child: for if thou beatest him with the rod, he shall not die. Thou shall beat him with the rod, and shall deliver his soul from hell." But today the US government charges people with child abuse if they spank their children, so most people are scared to even discipline their children today; yes, they're scared of being arrested and going to jail for child abuse. But what did God say, and who are we to listen to first God or man? And today there are so many of us that wonder why so many children, and plus the world itself, are like they are today. Now who enjoys being spanked? I know I didn't! But today I'm so grateful that I had a mother who would surely discipline me when I was wrong. And even though a lot of the times when I didn't want to listen to my mother back then, I still heard what she said, and most of the time, if not all the time, when she was correcting me, she was surely right and I was the one that was wrong, so I say, "Thanks, Mom!" *Now believe me, I have asked myself many times, just where would I be today if my mother didn't spank me as her way of correcting me, and all I seem to come up with is most likely in jail for the rest of my life, if not dead,* so once again do I say, "Thanks, Mom." Now while I was still going to Lore school, in less than a year after I had started seeing the dragon that so many times I truly did see. The state of Delaware's school district convinced my mother that I had a mental problem. They also told her that I was very hardheaded and wouldn't listen to them, saying that whenever they told me to sit down, I wouldn't sit. But you remember when I started telling you about the dragon I also told you that whenever I saw the red dragon, I didn't hear or see anything else but the dragon, and believe me, I didn't. Now along with them convincing my mother that I had a mental problem, they also convinced her to have me put in an institution. Yes, a mental hospital that went by the name of Governor Beacon Health Center that was located in Delaware City. Now my family soon moved from the Westside of Wilmington down to the Eastside, which we called Downtown, and the day after that I was placed in Governor Beacon, in 1970, I was only nine years old at the time. I now ask everyone from that time and age to tell me, really, how much wrong do you remember that a child could or would do back then? And I'm just sure your answer will be "Not anywhere near how much wrong children do today, would not you say?" One of my favorite lines I used to say to my mother all the time was, "*Mom, we used to be like angels compared to the children growing up today in the USA,* and that's because we would never do the kind of things children do today." Now after being put in Governor Beacon Health Center, I'd say by the time I was about twelve years of age, Governor Beacon put me on a medication called Thorazine, and they had me taking 200 mg of this medication three times a day. Now this is another time where I can show you how real, strong, and true God's love and Word truly, truly is and that, as He said, it will always stand. Now I'll start with saying that the first two times I was given the medication Thorazine while in Governor Beacon Health Center, I willingly took it for them, but this medicine had me so out of it that my face laid over my chest and I just sat like this for several hours as if I were lost in space. But after that, the first two times they gave it to me, the next time they did, God had also given me something else. Yes, He did; God also gave me enough sense to use my brain that He'd also given me for the better. So when they gave me the medication Thorazine to take once again, I came up with an idea. After I'd put the medicine in my mouth to swallow down my throat, instead of swallowing it to the bottom of my stomach, I caught it in my throat with my Adam's apple and held it there in my throat until after I left the cottage when the nurse was done with me, and then when I was back outside the cottage, I coughed the pill back up my throat from my Adam's apple and spit it out my mouth. So once again do I say that it couldn't have been anyone but God with me to give me such an idea that truly nothing else but worked for the four years that Governor Beacon Health Center had me taking it. Remember, I was only twelve years old when they started giving it to me to take, but also remember the idea that God had given me worked to keep it out of my human body that's first His temple. Now after having to take 200 mg of Thorazine three times a day for four years, I now take that it was against the law for them to up the dosage any more than what they were already giving me, for I'm sure that if they could have, they would have. But God's good, isn't He? Now I was once told by an older friend of mine that knew a little something about medications, and this friend told me that if I had continued taking the medication Thorazine at the amount of dosage that Governor Beacon was giving to me, the whole time they were giving it to me, today I wouldn't even have a brain, for by the time I had gotten out of Governor Beacon, the Thorazine would have burned my brains out. And you know what, going off how the medication Thorazine had me feeling after the first two times I'd taken, it makes me believe what my friend had told me was nothing but the truth without a doubt, which makes me also say once again, "God does protect His own," and with that, I also say that I'm living proof of that, and believe me, that's a fact. I got out of Governor Beacon Health Center at the age of sixteen in 1976. Now I believe being partly raised in an institution and not in a loving home with a loving family really hurt me a lot more than it helped me. I'm not trying to say my mother didn't love me for she did, and she loved all her children very, very much, but let us not forget how hard it was for a female back in the day. On top of that, it was even harder for a black woman, especially a black woman trying to raise a whole family by herself, am not I right? Now my mother had seven children; my grandmother raised two of them, and if I'm not mistaken, most grandmothers always want to play a part in raising their grandchildren. I know most grandmothers usually want to at least raise one of her grandchildren, right? I think that comes naturally, don't you? Another one of my sisters, my mother let a good friend of hers raise, and that wasn't because she didn't love or want her for, once again, she loved us all; no, she did it for two other reasons, and both of the reasons were out of love. Again, as I said, she loved all her children, but as I also said, it was very hard, as well as very expensive, for a black family back then and, once again, even harder for a black woman to do this by herself as my mother and so many other women had to do it back then, and there's so many others that still have to do today because so many men back then, as well as today, didn't or don't want to do their job of being "a real man" and a good husband and father after playing the part in making the child.

Let's not forget that no child ever asked to come into the world, and let us also not forget that God said the man was to till the ground. Now, as I said, there were two reasons my mother let her friend raise one of my sisters, and as the first one was for love, the second one was for love also, but this time, it was for how much my mother loved her friend and my sister also. You see, for some reason, her friend couldn't bear a child of her own. But my mother loved her so much that she let her raise my sister because it would help both my mother and her friend, plus my sister. Now everyone knows that all women look forward to one day having children of their own, right? And what's always been most girls first and favorite toy? A doll, right? So you see, my mother was giving her friend her first real doll baby that I'm sure she always wanted, but for some reason, couldn't make one on her own. Besides that, what women would love a child more than a woman that couldn't have one of her own besides the real mother of the child? And if you really look at the whole picture, you can't help but see that God was loving and helping everyone at the table as He always has and always will. Yes, He'll always be nothing but love, love, and more love, and the table does turn. Now, after getting out of Governor Beacon when I was sixteen, at the age of seventeen, I was right back in a boys' school called Ferris School for Boys in less than a year. I was put in Ferris School for Boys for fighting. Now I'm not trying to say fighting is good or right, for it's not. No, it's wrong, for God said we're to love all. But if I told you that it wouldn't be hard for one to survive in one of these youth or adult prisons and remain yourself without knowing how to fight to defend yourself and sometimes having to, I would be then lying to you, and no longer can I do that, for then would I first be lying to God, true? Believe me, there's no one that can really do that, for it's something that just can't be done. For as He's the Father, the Son, and also the Holy Ghost, He's first the breath of life, and that means that He's truly in us all, alright? Now after arriving at Ferris School for Boys, I was first placed in a tight, closed-in program of theirs that was called SVP. And while in this program, I started reading the Holy Bible, and believe me, I started reading it a lot for it helped very much to occupy my time, but also by reading it, it came to be the most fascinating book to me that's ever been written. It's surely the most fascinating book that I've ever read, and on top of that, it's also one of the only books that I ever read from beginning to end. You see, from being partly raised in an institution and boys' school, I was robbed of both my youth and my education, and today education is something we all very much need to survive in this world we live in. Now about six months later, I was moved from SVP into another program of theirs that was a little lighter, which they called STU. Now most people should know that children as young juveniles can and sometimes would tell some of the biggest of lies. For instance, when a new staff member would start working at Ferris and they didn't quite know all the rules yet, one of them would maybe ask one of us something like, "What time are you guys supposed to be in bed?" We'd usually tell them a lie; yes, we'd come back with something like "We don't have to crash out until eleven o'clock" when we knew we were supposed to be in bed at nine o'clock. But I remember one time when a man started working there by the name of Elder Jones. Now once Reverend Jones wanted to know what our bedtime was, and when he asked us that question, not one of us lied to him; in fact, we all told him exactly what he wanted to know. But the funny thing about it wasn't that we didn't lie to him about it; in fact, we all told him nothing but the truth. No, the funny thing was that when bedtime came around, he didn't even have to ask us to go. No, he didn't, for when it was bedtime, we all got up like soldiers and went right to bed. And that night I set up half the night just wondering why we didn't treat him as we had treated all the others, and believe me, at the time, I just couldn't understand why, but I do now though! Yes, I do, for I later found out that Mr. Jones was a real pastor who's also truly a child of God, so here we're back again with "God protects His own." Now in no time at all, me and Rev. Jones came to be the best of friends; in fact, Rev. Elder Jones is the only pastor that I ever met that I know was a real pastor, for he was also the only one I ever met that whenever I was around him, I could actually feel God there with us in Rev. Jones. I guess that was something else that attracted me to him and also made me love him as I did and also makes me now say, "May he rest in peace." Now I know in this world today we have a lot of people who are claiming to be pastors, but we must be careful for everyone claiming to be one isn't. Take my situation at Ferris with Rev. Jones for instance; believe me, the only reason we treated him with nothing but respect as we did, plus with the kind of respect we treated him with, was because he was truly a child of God, and once again, God protects His own, so He wouldn't let us treat him with nothing else but respect and wouldn't let one do him wrong in any kind of way. I mean, we couldn't even tell him a lie with him being one that belonged to God. So I ask you all once again to believe me for here I tell nothing but the truth. Yes, believe me, and by just reading the Bible, you really couldn't do anything else but learn that what I'm telling you is true, for when you read the Bible, you're then reading the true intelligence of God, who's truly the Genius of genius. And why's that, I'm sure some ask? And I say because it was God that created our main three elements—heaven, earth, and sea—and everything else of life was also created by He. On top of that, He did it all in six days, didn't He? Yes, He did so that on the seventh day, He could rest from all His creating, you see. And that alone makes me say if that's not both totally amazing and also God, then you tell me what and who is, would you! Now in the book of Genesis 1:31 that after all this took place, it was said, "And God saw everything that He had made, and behold, it was very good. And the evening and morning were the sixth day." Also everything God made and did, He made and did for a reason. For Jehovah, yes, God, who's truly our Heavenly Father, makes nothing for nothing and nothing with nothing. For instance, let's take the Holy Bible, yes, the Word of God, and believe me, it was written for a reason. I mean, did you know each letter in the words *holy* and *Bible* stand for other whole words of their own? Well, yes, they do, and here we go again with understanding the intelligence of God a little better than we already do, so again take the Holy Bible and check this out. Believe me, just as God Himself, you'll find it unbelievable too; yes, also just as God Himself, it too is very, very real and very, very true just like me and you and you.

HOLY BIBLE

Here Our Lord Yields Basic Instructions Before Leaving Earth

Now isn't that fascinating? As I said earlier, everything God does or did, He did for a reason, even named His book of instructions Holy Bible. Now as God once told me, I ask you to please believe me, for it is so true, yes, that He's been a Cloud over me all my life. Now let me share another incident that once happened in my life with you, for it too also shows God's love to me by being a cloud of protection over me. And with that, I say from the bottom of my heart that our God's love does and did protect me as His own. Now when I was that eight-year-old that I once was when I went to Lore school, at the time my grandmother lived between 2nd and 3rd in Clayton Street, which was across the street from another public park named at that time, Clayton Street Park. Now on both sides of 2nd and Clayton Street, as well as all the way around the park, there were lots and lots of trees, and because of this, every fall, all these trees would always leave lots and lots of leaves just everywhere; I'm sure you know what I mean. Yes, they'd fall all over the street as well as all the houses on that block. Now when I was in my mid to late twenties, my grandmother still lived on Clayton Street; in fact, one of my blood sisters owns that house now and still lives there in it. Anyway, one fall, I told my grandmother that year I would go up on her roof and clean the leaves off it for her. The problem was that when she phoned me asking if I would still do the job for her, I said yes, I would as I said I would, but for some reason at the time, my ladder somehow got broken. Now I didn't let that stop me from doing for my grandmother what I said I would do, but when I went to do the job, because of my ladder being broken I only had half a ladder to work with, so I had to climb the half of the ladder that I had from the ground up to the porch rooftop and then pull the ladder up to the porch roof and set it up so I could climb up to the house rooftop. Now when I did, I realized there was a slight slant in the porch roof. After I did set it all up and was climbing up the ladder to the house rooftop as I started trying to take one of my feet off the ladder to step on to the rooftop, the slant in the porch roof caused the ladder to slip as I was stepping off it on to the housetop. I then fell from the top of the house down to the ground, landing on solid concrete. Now the amazing thing about that was that after having the worst fall I ever had in my life, when I gotten up from the ground, I realized that I didn't even need a Band-Aid. No, I didn't. I just asked my grandmother to hand me a paper towel, and I then just held it against the back of my leg where I had picked up a scratch from the fall. Now someone tell me that God didn't tell Michael and Gabriel to go catch me, His son! I also now walk with a cane because of another accident that once happened to me. May I also share it with you so I can also once again share the good news about God's loving grace with you too. Now one day I was on my way to a corner store when a guy pulled up next to me with a carload of others. He then asked me if I knew where he and his friends could get some crack cocaine? This was a Caucasian young man, and because of his race and also because we were in a very bad black neighborhood, as well as the information he was asking me for and once again because of the color of his and his companions' skin, I was really pretty scared for them. I mean, with me knowing what could end up happening to them here if they tried to get this on their own, can you blame me for being scared for them? Don't you think you would have been kind of scared too? So I said to them, why not let me go and get it for you? For I also believe if I didn't volunteer to do it for them, I'm sure they would have kept on looking for their selves until they found it, and who knows what else they may have found before it or with it! The guy who asked me then agreed to let me go and get it for them, and as he put his money in one of my hands, the money that I was going to the store with was in my other hand. Now after I had gone and gotten for him what he wanted, I turned back around and went back to the car to give it to him. And as I said, my money was still in my other hand, and when I dropped the drugs in his hand that I'd gotten for him instead of him thanking me, showing his appreciation for what I had just done for him and his friends, he instead snatched my money out of my other hand and took off in his car. Now here we once again see very clearly that God meant very much what He said when He said,

"*Never will I leave you and never will I forsake you.*" Now before the guy could get away from me in his car, I leaped onto it and was holding on to it with my right hand from the backdoor window frame and had my left arm in the front window, trying to get my hand around his neck or the steering wheel, hoping to force him to drive the car off the road. But unfortunately, he got the car doing about ninety miles an hour and then ran me into a Blazer to force me off his car. And in the end, they had to fly me in a helicopter from Riverside of North Wilmington to the Christiana Hospital that was located in Newark, Delaware. Now after all that I've shared here with you so far today, you should clearly see without any reason of doubt that God never left me, nor did He forsake me. No, He never let me down, and so many times it seemed that there was nobody else there but God to truly help me up, and just because faithfully He being there every time I needed Him to pick me up and, yes, dust me off, He was there, is the main reason I'm still here today to share with you just how good God is, and believe me, if you would accept Him just like I have accepted Him, He would also be there to help you up and dust you off if you ever happen to fall, and with that, I once again say that it's just so true that God does protect His own! Now I started smoking cigarettes at the age of sixteen, but through the power of God and Chantix, it's something I haven't done now for over seventeen years, and yes, all credit goes to God, my heavenly Father, and Chantix and surely not me, for God gave me all the strength I needed, but without God, I didn't seem to have enough strength to overcome such a bad habit on my own. And a second time the credit first goes to God, the Genius of geniuses; yes, He's the first genius who also made a genius out of the person whom God chose to be the inventor of Chantix, which helped me and, I'm sure, so many others to break the bad habit of smoking cigarettes. Now over the years, I also became a crackhead as we called them back then, and that's how I knew the kind of danger and chance those young Caucasians would have been taking if they went and tried to buy the crack cocaine they wanted on their own. Yes, I knew because I was a user too. I also knew a lot of the dealers of it in Riverside, as well as a lot of the users. Now I'm sorry for it, but once again at the time, I was a user too, so I also knew what could happen to them in Riverside if they tried to get it themselves. Think about what happened to me after I went and got it for them because I didn't want to see any of them get hurt. But still even after I brought it back to them, the guy driving the car snatched my money out of my hand, and then when I was hanging on his car, trying to get my money back, he ran me into a Blazer to knock me off the car. Now if they would do that to me, what do you think one of the other users or dealers may have done to them if I had let them go and try to get it for themselves? Believe me, it's really not the person doing it, but it's the addiction you get from the drug. Again, believe me, for I do know, for I was once an addict too. I'm now on disability, which is partly from the damage done to me when the guy ran me into the Blazer and knocked me off the car. And before God helped me by removing the addiction I had gotten from using crack cocaine. You know sometimes I would blow my whole disability check up in smoke in 2 days and then wonder how I was going to eat for the rest of the month after just spending all I had for the month in just 2 or 3 days, and believe me, if it wasn't for God, I really don't know what I would have done! But what I do know is, the same way God helped me remove that bad habit and so many other problems I had, because He loved me. He will also help you and anyone else with their problems that truly comes to Him for any help they might need, which includes you too, and that's nothing but the truth. Yes, God will help any one of us with any problem we may have at any time and on any day you may be having that problem if you just ask Him, trust Him, and let Him, for as He said to Father Abraham years ago still stands, and He still stands by it, yes, those most powerful words; He said, "Is there anything I can't do?" And is there? Tell me, for this time I ask you! Well, just in case you don't know, let me assure you that no, there's not. Now there's a lot of things we can't do, but once again, I ask everyone to please believe me when I say that no, there's nothing that God can't do, a fact that's oh so real and oh so true. Remember that old saying "Prayer does work?" Well, it's nothing but the plain truth. But you know there's also something else that really takes me out. And what's that, I guess you ask? Do you know or remember that other old saying that's been flying around the world about forever? Yes, "time does fly." Wouldn't you say it does? The funny thing about it, though, is that it's so true, you know? Believe me, time does fly, and that's even when you're not having fun. And, why do I say this? Well, for one, it seemed just like a twinkle of an eye after I'd turned seventeen and gotten out of Ferris School for Boys, the youth prison I had been in; just like that, I was in Gander Hill, an adult prison, once again for third-degree assault, again fighting. I guess I was one that just couldn't stand it when another would put their hands on me, intending to hurt me, so whenever one did, I made him very sorry that he tried and also made very clear to him that he best not ever do it again. But the thing was, even though they always hit me first, it seemed that I was always the one that ended up in jail, being at the short end of the stick, and that was because even though my opponents would always put their hands on me first, still by the time the police would get there to break it up, they would always find me on the top doing the banging, so I would always get the slam against the wall, followed by the handcuffs and most of my opponents either got the stretcher or was lucky and got released and would be able to just walk away. Another thing that seemed to take me a long time to learn—but I did finally learn—that once you were in the system, it was very, very hard to get out. Now one time after doing several months in jail waiting for court, I was finally released on a one-year probation sentence. Now when it was finally over, I went to the probation office to get my papers that verified that my probation was completed, and as I was exiting the building, a police officer was also entering, and as we were passing by each other, we accidentally bumped into each other. I guess he wanted to get in just as badly as I wanted to get out, you know? Anyway, the officer looked at me and then asked, "Is your name Kevin Moss?" So I said, "Yes, it is, Officer. Is there a problem, sir?" The police officer then said, "I'm sorry, but I'm afraid there is, Mr. Moss, for it seems we have a warrant for your arrest for failing to pay a $250 fine from thirteen years ago." So I say to the officer, "I'm sorry, but you must have the wrong person, Officer, for I don't know what you're talking about, and believe me, I didn't!" For whenever I was sentenced for something, I would always take the jail or probation sentence and never took fines as my sentence for I know I didn't have the money to pay them and to take such a sentence when you know you didn't have the money to pay was stupid to me because when you would get in trouble again, and most of the time we did, and would end up back in front of a judge for it would all come back on you. First what you were being arrested for then and then what you were arrested for the last time and didn't pay your fine, so in the long run, it was even worse than it was before, so again to take fines as my sentence was stupid and something that I didn't do. I would also make that very clear to my public defender. On top of that, remember as I said in the beginning of this story, the only reason I was at the probation office that day in the first place was to get the completion papers from my probation officer, and I had the papers with me, for again I was leaving, correct? Now it's a fact that in the State of Delaware, you can't get off probation until all fines are paid, and since I just got off probation, I obviously didn't have any fines to pay, again, correct? So to me, the real question is, where was this fine the officer was saying I had just five minutes ago? For once again, I just got off probation. But whether I did or not, the next thing you know is, I'm locked up again, and this time for what? I just don't know. Now this all took place in the month of April, so surely I was pretty much in summer clothing. But after they had once again incarcerated me, they held me in jail for nine months waiting for court. Now that was three months in the Gander Hill Prison, located in Wilmington, Delaware and then three months in the Smyrna Prison, located in Southern Delaware, and three months in Georgetown Prison, which is located even further south in Delaware. Now when I was finally taken to court for this $250 fine at the time, we were in the month of December, Georgetown Prison had me transported to the Wilmington Superior Court, with me not having on a sweater, jacket, or coat; in fact, I didn't even have on a hat. Now when the judge entered the court and took his seat, he first looked over the papers before him that were pertaining to my case, and after reading them, he couldn't believe himself what he had just read and snapped. Yes, he snapped, only he snapped on them, not on me, for as I said from the jump, I didn't even know what they were talking about the whole time, and believe me, I didn't. The judge then said very loudly, "You're telling me you've held this man in jail for nine months now for a $250 fine from thirteen years ago?" The judge also said, "This man should have been released from prison for this over six months ago!" The prison officers were then very angry after this, for again as I said, the judge had gotten on them, not me. Plus, as I also said, in this whole situation, I never did anything in the first place, and one more time, I didn't, besides being in the wrong place at the wrong time. For as I said before, if the fine that the officer said I owed which I was being charged with for not paying never existed in the first place, as I asked you my readers before, if it did, then where was the fine just five minutes before I got off probation? The prison guards then took me back to the Georgetown Prison from the Wilmington Courthouse which is in my hometown, when I was innocent of it all in the first place; now explain that to me. Now when we did get back to the prison, the authorities there got me to sign my name on a piece of paper then gave me my belongings, which wasn't nothing but the keys to my home for the rest of them were already on my back. Then one of the prison guards walked me to the front gate, kicked the fence open, and told me to get out. Now I think I've made it very clear that I'm from upstate and know nothing about downstate; besides that I knew that I was in Georgetown so I really didn't know which way I was supposed to go, whether I was going upstate or downstate; you know what I mean? But lucky for me, God is a man of His word, meaning never did He leave me and never did He forsake me for he gave me enough sense to know that if I wanted to get back upstate, I would have to find my way to Rt. 13. Now that day, the sun was blazing in my face, which is the last thing that I remember besides looking down at my wrist watch and seeing that at the moment, it was 12:30 p.m. The next thing I know was, I was hearing a voice that was saying to me, "Get up, get up, get up, my child." After hearing the voice, my eyes began to open back up, but all I saw were car and truck headlights coming straight at me as if they were going to run me over, which had me scared, yes, I was so scared that I started hollering for my life. But again, thanks to God and lucky for me that I was far enough on the side of the road on the bike trail that all the vehicles whose headlights I was seeing just flew by me without even one of them hitting me. God's good, isn't He? At the time I also realized that it was a lot colder and also pitch-black dark at that time besides the stars in the sky, which meant the sun had gone down, so it was between 5:00 to 7:00 p.m. Now after I had fully come to, I also realized that I had a seizure while I was out of it, and that may have been what took me out in the first place, if you know what I mean. But either way it goes really didn't make any difference for I had been lying out on the road for at least five, to seven hours at the time, so I must thank God again, and believe me, I do, for to me, I was really lucky to even still be alive for once again I was still outside in December in the cold without having on a sweater, jacket, or coat. You know it's really hard to believe that when the State of Delaware did this; we were in the month of December, and I was in their Georgetown Prison. Believe me, I was and then had to walk all the way back to Wilmington from Georgetown for something I never did in the first place. But by the love, mercy, and grace of God, I did succeed. Yes, it's all just so hard to believe, but whatever our problem may be, Jesus Christ is all we need. Yes, it's so unbelievable but also such a thrill that after all I had gone through, I'm still here; yes, I'm still here and alive. Yet it couldn't have ever happened, and I survive—meaning still be alive but through nothing else but the love of God. And by that love, I'm still here after all I have been through, and it all takes me right back to something I said in the beginning of the book, which is, God does protect what belongs to Him! And believe me, it's such a blessing, which I say from the bottom of my heart. So now after God had opened my eyes back up, He gave me the strength I needed to roll over from my back to my hands and knees and after that happened while I was still on my hands and knees, I, all of a sudden, heard a voice that said to me, "Turn to your right," and I knew it had to be the voice of God talking to me once again. Now when I did as He said and did turn my face to the right of me, I was then looking up a steep hill that was to the right of me. And when I looked up the hill, I saw a picnic table at the top of it. God then gave me the strength I needed to get up from my hands and knees and stand on my feet. Now after getting up from the ground and standing on my feet, which first stand on God's feet, I walked up the hill until I'd gotten to the top of it. And when I got there, I leaned against it with my backside and leaned forward with my upper body, putting my hands between my legs, trying to warm them up for my hands as well as; my whole body was very, very cold after being outside for so long. I then told myself that I felt warmer when I was walking down Rt. 13, so yes, I walked back down the hill and once again started walking north on Rt. 13. Yes, I started moving my feet from left to right, going north, feeling inside my heart and saying in my mind, *If I can just make it back home safely, that would be great*, and from there, I just kept walking, until, all of a sudden, I heard a car horn blowing in my ear, and when I looked behind me, I felt a little nervous, or should I say scared, for there was someone sitting in a car on the side of the road a few feet behind me, trying to get my attention by once again blowing his horn several times at me. You know, I almost felt like the whole world was stalking me down. But I then said to myself, *What are you scared for, I mean, didn't God make sure you got this far? And on top of that, this might be a ride all the way home!* So I then walked over to the car, and when I got there, a pretty nice guy said to me, "Just where are you going at this time of night or so early in the morning as cold as it is? I hope not far." And I said, "I'm going back upstate to Wilmington where I come from." I then told him all that had happened to me starting from the day before. And he then said, "I'm sorry, I can't take you all the way back to Wilmington, but I will take you as far as I can if you'll just hop in, my friend." I then got into his car, and we took off, going north up Rt. 13. I'll say he then drove me about two or three miles and then pulled the car back over to the side of the road and said, "This is about as far as I can go." He then let me out of the car and gave me a brotherly handshake with a smile and said, "I hope you make it okay." I then got out of his car, thanked him, and took off, walking again up Rt. 13 while remembering something my mother always said, which was "Beggars can't be choicy," and from how his ride helped, my feet feel so much better than they felt when I first got in his car with him, which made me have to once more say. Mom, you were right again. When I was done thinking about all this, I guess I had been walking about a half an hour or forty-five minutes, and all of a sudden, I heard a horn blowing once again. Now the big surprise in this was when I turned around and looked back to see who was blowing their horn at me this time, I couldn't believe it when I saw that it was the same guy that helped me with the ride the first time, back again. So when I hopped back in the car with him, he said, "I see you're still walking, my friend." And I said, "I have no choice until I get home." He then said, "Now I still can't drive you all the way back to Wilmington, but once again, I'll drive you as far as I can." And all I could do was thank him over and over, again and again. Now I guess this time he drove me about three or four miles more than he did the first time. My friend then stopped the car, let me get out of it, and then said, "Goodbye, my friend, and again I hope you make it to your destination." He then made a right turn into a construction site where they were doing some building. I believe they were building an apartment complex there. At least that's what it looked like to me, but whether it was or wasn't really didn't matter for I was on the road on my way on a new day. Yes, I was back on my hike, and that's for sure, alright? Believe me, at times I really felt like I was on a natural high by the grace of God, and that made me feel a whole lot better, for I must say. As I said before, after my friend took off, he turned into a construction site, and that proves that he was telling the truth when he said he couldn't drive me all the way back to Wilmington, for as he also said the first time he had to go to work but first he had to go to a hardware store for the company he worked for, which must have been the truth, for after he let me out of his car the first time, he made a U-turn from going north and turned around and started driving south, and then after he had picked me up the second time, as I told you, he turned into a construction site, and I'm sure if he had gone on and driven me home, he would have lost his job. But still I must and do thank him with all my heart for both rides that he gave me that day, for they both helped me in every way. So do I say, God bless him for all his help and brotherly love that he showed me that day. Anyway, just like a twinkle after I had started walking back to Wilmington after my new friend had let me out, it seemed just like that I was home unlocking and entering the front door, walking in the house, and all thanks goes to both

God, my heavenly spouse, and my nice new friend who gave me the two rides that he did. So through God, who gave me the strength that I needed to make such a long walk as I did and for not allowing my body to freeze up when I was earlier laid out on the ground from the seizure I'd had, and one more time do I also thank my friend for the two helping rides he gave me. Amen. Now after this had all happened, on another day, I was telling another friend of mine all about it, and when I was finished, he then asked me, "Well, how did you get over the bridge that day?" And I came back with, "What bridge? I don't remember seeing or going over any bridge, and believe me, I didn't." My friend then said, "Well, you have to go over the bridge to get from downstate back upstate and vice versa." But again I don't remember going over any bridge! And then one day I started thinking about what my friend had said again, and I asked myself, *Well, how did I get over the bridge then?* Well, all I could come up with was, it must have been God once again. Yes, God obviously got me over, under, or around for I surely got from one side to the other, and I surely got home, right? Besides that, remember what my friend said; I had to have gotten over the bridge some kind of way, and believe me once again, God's just that good. He's always there, and He does protect His own, and you know what, it's just so good to be God's, and you can take that to the bank! And please don't forget what God once said to one of His servants, which was, "*Is there anything I can't do?*" And is there? You tell me. And now let me tell you one more thing before I forget. Also, while I was still in the Georgetown Prison, I came to realize that God had also given me another gift, yes, the gift of writing poetry, which has come to be so easy for me, which is another reason that I know it was a gift from God. I mean, just with the twinkle of an eye, I can write some of the most beautiful poems. Now once upon a time, after my mother had two strokes after I had gotten out of prison, I was once again living with her, and while there, I was also nursing her. And one day while she was in her bedroom asleep, I was in the living room going over my first book of poetry, which I had named *Poems of Love and Life Coming from the Heart*. And as I was going over some of the poems in it, trying to find any mistakes I may have made when I was first writing them, I wanted to try to correct any wrong spelling I found. Anyway, as I was reading one of them, for some reason, as I read it, I started crying like a baby and water was running down my face like a waterfall, but I couldn't understand why all this was happening. So I ask myself, *What are you crying for? You've read these poems over a thousand times!* So I once again ask myself, *So what are you crying for?* I then got up from the sofa and walked over to the dining room, and at that very moment, God started talking to me, and He answered the question that I had just several times asked myself of why I was crying by saying, "Because I wanted to let you know that I'm the author but decided to use you as my tool!" Now at the end of all the poems I was going over ended with "*By Kevin Moss,*" but after God had spoken to me, telling me that He would be the author of my book, all of a sudden, another phrase just popped into my head as someone had punched me in it, and you'll read that phrase at the end of every one of the poems I've written here God is the author and not me, but I'm His tool.

Yes, Here a Tool of God's I am!

Saying one more time that it's so, so true that,
yes, God does protect His own!

The Lord of Host is with us; the God of Jacob is our refuge. Selah.
Come, behold the works of the Lord; what
desolation He has made in the earth.
He maketh wars to cease unto the end of the earth; He
breaketh the bow and cutteth the spear in sunder;
"He burneth the chariot in the fire. Be
still and know that I am God."
I will be exalted among the heathen; I will be exalted in the earth.
The Lord of Host is with us; the God of Jacob is our refuge. Selah.
(Psalm 46:7–11)

Remember, To God, all lives matter!

LOVE,

LOVE,

AND

MORE

LOVE

With Love, Love, and More Love!

Love, Love, and more Love I'd truly like to have.
Yes, I would, for it would make me happy,
happy, happy, and oh so glad.
I just know Love, Love, and more Love would
put a happy smile on my face.
And then inside my heart I wouldn't feel so sad or oh so bad.
Now I know with faith that Love, Love, and more Love
makes One oh so glad, for Love is truly an Ace.
And at the very same time, it removes all frowns from One's face.
I truly hate the look of a frown on One's face.
And that's because it shows that you're oh so
sad and it also slows down your pace.
So believe me, Love, Love, and more Love is something we all
want and truly need to have. For if One has Love, they truly
have God, and through God, we can have it all as it's been said.
So once more do I tell you that God is Love, Love,
and more Love who's at your every call.
Also with His pure Love, Love, Love, He'll pick you
up and wipe you off if you ever happen to fall.
So if I can't have God the Father, God the
Son, and God the Holy Ghost.
Who's Love, Love, Love do I truly call,
Then I'd rather have nothing, just nothing at all!!

***By** Jehovah* THROUGH THE HEART, MIND,
AND LEFT HAND OF ***Kevin Moss***

Jesus saith unto him, I am the way, the truth and the life: no man cometh unto the Father, but by Me.

—JOHN 14:6

"WITH LOVE, LOVE, AND MORE LOVE"

Beautiful, Unique, and True

So beautiful are all the lovely things God made
for all of we, and it, nature called He.
As of every beautiful flower growing with all the lovely trees.
Some grow in the summer, winter, spring, and fall, and a nice cool
breeze blows through them all. How about all the big rivers, small
ponds, and unique streams that connect back to the first sea?
They're all just so beautiful and unique to me. Are they not to you?
Yes, Tell Me Aren't They ALL Just Beautiful, Unique, and True?
It's so unique how God made so many mountains and falls.
Yes, from many rocks and stones He made them all.
Yes, fall after fall does His water flow straight down
those rocks; all, all, and all down does it go.
He also allowed the sun in the day, the moon and stars
at night down on we all to shine their light oh so bright.
And through God do they shine their light down on all of
we as God shines His Love on us too, do not you see?
And oh so brightly with He do they shine; yes, they do, they
do, they do just shine, shine, shine on Both Me and You.
Yes, They Shine So Beautiful, Unique, and True Do
They Shine for us all, yes, again, on Me and You.
For true is our God and true He's always been and true He'll always be.
Yes, just as true as it was, He who made for
us all the Heavens, Earth, and Sea.
Believe me, everything God made, He made
it oh so Good, this do not you see?
Sure, you can see that it's all Beautiful, Unique,
and True through, through, and through.
And That Includes All of We, Meaning Once Again
Both Me and You for Just Like Our God and Savior
WE TOO ARE ALSO JUST SO BEAUTIFUL,
UNIQUE, AND TRUE!

By** Jehovah* THROUGH THE HEART, MIND, AND LEFT HAND OF ***Kevin Moss

"When He prepared the heavens, I was there: when He set a compass upon the face of the depth: When He established the clouds above: when He strengthened the fountains of the deep: When He gave to the sea His decree, that the waters should not pass His Commandment: when He appointed the foundations of the earth. Then I was by Him, as one brought up With Him: and I was daily His delight, rejoicing always before Him; Rejoicing in the habitable part of His earth; and my delights were with the sons men."

—PROVERBS 8:27–31

A Man!

JEHOVAH is the name of God, our Heavenly
Father, who's also our creator.
And we're to follow His commands.
This was proven in our most time of need, for then He
stood nailed to a cross and still does He stand.
On the sixth day of His creating, He said to His first
Son, yes, to our Lord Jesus Christ, He did say.
"Let Us Make Man in Our Own Image,
According to Our Likeness."
Truly does this mean Man is really not flesh.
But spirit, which is God's image and likeness.
And if I'm not mistaken, God made Man for
Himself and then made Woman for Man.
He then said Man would be the head of the
household and the Woman his right arm.
The problem is, so many boys misinterpreted
what God meant when He said "HEAD."
Believe me, He didn't mean for Man to dominate
the Woman, who's to be his right arm.
No, He didn't mean that, for remember, even
though they're two they're truly only one!
What God meant was for Man to be there in all
her times of need, as He's been here for ours.
In other words, yes, man's to stand tall!
By being dominant in making sure that his children
and wife have a roof over their heads.
Yes, that at all times they're fed, clothed
and have a roof over their heads.
And remember, even if the roof is nothing but a
tent, it's still a roof that's over their heads.
That makes a Man. It's also being a Man and
any Male being like He is a Man!

So here we Men must follow our Lord Jesus Christ by doing God's Will and following His Command in Being *A MAN, A MAN, A REAL MAN!*

By *Jehovah* THROUGH THE HEART, MIND, AND LEFT HAND OF ***Kevin Moss***

And God said, Let Us make man in Our Image, after Our Likeness: and let them have dominion over the fish of the sea, and over the fowl of the air, and over the cattle, and over all the *Earth*, and over every creeping-thing that creeps upon the *Earth*. So God created man in His Own Image, in the Image of God created He him; male and female created He them. And God blessed them, and God said unto them, *be fruitful, and multiply, and replenish the earth and subdue it.*

—GENESIS 1:26–28 (emphasis added)

Thou Shall Not Kill!

By God were we all given life and life were
we given from He with love.
Yes, with love did God give us life, and we're
to live this life as He, by showing love!
Truly are we to live this life filled with love and surely not hate.
Yes, let us live by God's laws with love and not by Santa's hate.
Showing love is God's will, and remember,
everyone, also a law of God's so truly is
"THOU SHALL NOT KILL!"
We all had or have a mother who carried us
before delivering us into the world.
And after God gave us life, to most our mothers, with
love, we became her precious, precious pearl.
Now the pearls that shine we find in shells.
But we find the precious ones in the heart
of mothers, and surly not hell!
SO THOU SHALL NOT KILL!
Believe me, love, love, and more love will get
you nothing but over the hump.
But life can be so hard at times it may feel like bump, bump, bump.
Yes, so hard it can be that it feels like bump,
bump, and more bump, bump, bump!
But still it's love that's the key of life and not
the opposite of love, which is hate.
For love is life and hate is death and death is the worst.
Yes, it is as life with love so truly is the best.
And with that do I say may God's laws and
commands always be in our heart.
Yes, may they always be in our heart that we follow
His laws, and commands doing His will.
Now once again do I say what was once said by He,
which was His law and will, and it'll always be.
THOU SHALL NOT KILL!

By** Jehovah* THROUGH THE HEART, MIND, AND LEFT HAND OF ***Kevin Moss

From whence come wars and fighting among you? Come they not hence, even of your lusts that war in your members? You lust, and have not: you kill, and desire to have, and cannot obtain: you fight and war, yet you have not, because you ask not. You ask, and you receive not, because you ask amiss, that you may consume it upon your lusts. You adulterers and adulteresses, know you not that the friendship of the world is enmity with God? Whosoever therefore will be a friend of the world is enmity of God.

—JAMES 4:1–4

God Doesn't Like Ugly!

It's not right to cry of pain when you're really not
hurt or put another down and not help one up.
That's like instead of making one feel clean with
love, with hate you make them feel like dirt.
So believe me, believe me, believe me, Love, Love,
Love truly is the key, and besides that,
GOD DOESN'T LIKE UGLY!
So don't speak to another at such a high tone of voice.
Don't do that. No, you really shouldn't for showing
disrespect just isn't the right choice.
Just do as God said to, and treat others
as you want them to treat you.
For that's showing Love, true, and you can't beat that, can you?
No, you can't, for Love, Love, and more Love is just the right key.
Yes, it is and one more time I ask you to believe me.
Please believe me, believe me, believe me, yes, again believe me.
GOD DOESN'T LIKE UGLY!
So always remember you-al, we all, we all, yes, we all
come together no matter what race, creed, or color.
For we're all, yes, we're all human beings, which
means we're all sisters and brothers!
DO YOU KNOW WHAT I MEAN?
Yes, that, we truly are no matter what race, creed, or color you are.
So too you all I end with, remember, remember
and never forget, but always remember.
Remember that Love, Love, and more Love is the key.
ALSO REMEMBER AND DON'T EVER FORGET
THAT GOD DOESN'T LIKE UGLY!

***By** Jehovah* THROUGH THE HEART, MIND,
AND LEFT HAND OF ***Kevin Moss***

There are six things that the Lord, hates—actually seven things that He does not like: First and foremost, pride. Second, dishonesty. Third, taking advantage of innocent people. Fourth, always devising wicked schemes. Fifth, being in a hurry to sin some more. Sixth, falsifying reports in court. Seventh, sowing suspicion among friends.

—PROVERBS 6:16–19

With His and My Strength I'll Make It

I know it's much of a climb, but until I get
to the top, climbing I shall go.
Yes, I'm walking up that narrow path to the
entrance gate of the heavens high.
And through the blood and love of my Lord Jesus
Christ, and having faith in He, I'm sure to get by.
I know with faith, through His and my
strength, I'll make it on a natural high.
God never said it would always be cream and cake; but still
I love God just that much for God's just that great.
Yes, our God is so Wonderful and Great for it's through
His breath that we have Life and live on this date.
And through His first Son, Jesus Christ, do we live in He.
On top of that, it's through the Breath and
Strength of His that we were truly set free.
So may we all hold on to He with all our might do I say.
So on those days that it seems you just can't take, don't give
up hope, no, just trust in God for He's just that great.
Believe me, with His and your strength, you'll
make it for God loves us all the same way.
So let us all keep climbing up, yes, up, up we go every single day.
And always remember, you may have a fall here
or there and it just may not seem fair.
But also remember and never forget that He that
really, really cares will always be there.
And with that, may we all believe that one day in heaven
with God, our Heavenly Father, we shall surely sit.
I guess you now say, how or why do I
make a statement as this to you?
For one I know, and I also believe it too, that with His and
my strength, getting back home to heaven one day I'll do.
But the question I now ask, I ask to you and all the world, which is,
WHAT ABOUT YOU?

By** Jehovah* THROUGH THE HEART, MIND, AND LEFT HAND OF ***Kevin Moss

Then said Jesus unto His disciples, If any man will come after Me, let him deny himself, and take up his cross, and follow Me. For whosoever will save his life shall lose it: and whosoever will lose his life for My sake shall find it. For what is a man profited, if he shall gain the whole world, and lose his own soul, or what shall a man give in exchange for his soul?

—MATTHEW 16:24–26

It's Not about Money, but All about Love

It's not about money, no, it's not, it's all about Love,
for God is Love, who sits up high above.
Yes, *Jehovah*, our God, does sit high up above
with Love, Love, and more Love.
Yes, high up above He does sit, and there He watches
we such an evil world tear its self apart bit by bit.
It's really such a shame how so many in the
world today just think they're so cool.
But believe me, anyone in love with money, a plain
piece of paper, and not in Love with God is a fool.
Yes, believe me for what I tell you here today is
sent down to me from high up above.
Yes, just to tell you all with Love, Love, and more Love.
Truly He's *Jehovah*, yes, God, but it seems to
me the world just doesn't understand.
No, it seems that not one understands but His first
Son, Jesus Christ, what a man, what a man!
Now something He told me to tell you, I'm sure you heard before.
Yes, I'm repeating the words once coming from the mouth
of our Lord Jesus Christ, saying to we the world.
Yes, I'll tell you all once more.
Remember, Jesus once said to all of we the world
that the love of money is the root of all evil.
Now I ask you all to believe me for what
I say comes from He above.
And it's going out to all just like a loud whistle of Love.
And what's whistled now is the same thing
that was whistled back then,
Which is that it's not about money but all
about Love again, again, and again.

By** **Jehovah THROUGH THE HEART, MIND,
AND LEFT HAND OF ***Kevin Moss***

He who loves silver shall not be satisfied with silver; nor he who loves abundance with increase:

This is also vanity.

—ECCLESIASTES 5:10

He who trusts in his riches shall fall: but the righteous shall flourish as a branch.

—PROVERBS 11:28

Paper and Fire Just Don't Mix

You know, our world seems so wrapped up around paper today!
Plus, in every way it seems to be getting hotter
and hotter in this world, wouldn't you say?
And believe me, it really is, for there's no escape
of the climate change, in any way!
No, there's no escape, so one day we'll all be
bowing down to He the exact same way.
And believe me, everyone at that time we'll all be
judged by He, meaning both you and me.
But before that time gets here, I think we all better understand this:
Paper and Fire Just Don't Mix!
Now we find in the book of 1 Timothy 6:6–7 serving
God, by doing right makes a person rich.
Yes, by giving one contentment, courage, and hope, get it?
We brought nothing into this world, and it's
certain that we'll take nothing out.
And please believe me, even if God would let you take all the money
in the world with you, before you're even a quarter ways down to
where you're going, it would be gone, yes, gone,
just going up in smoke like paper sticks.
Yes, It Really, Really Would, for Once Again
Paper and Fire Just Don't Mix!

***By** Jehovah* THROUGH THE HEART, MIND,
AND LEFT HAND OF ***Kevin Moss***

Go too now, you rich men, weep and howl for your miseries that shall come upon you. Your riches are corrupted, and your garments are moth-eaten. Your gold and silver is cankered; and the rust of them shall be a witness against you, and shall eat your flesh as it were fire.

—JAMES 5:1–3

It's God's Way or the Highway

You know life is a two-way and not a one-way street,
Which means in life there's two different ways we can go.
Yes, we have a choice of two different directions
we can go, which is up or down!
Just two, as right and wrong, left or right, and good or bad,
which will always take you up or down safe and sound.
Yes, two directions have been given to both me and you,
along with all the rest that make the world go round.
Down, down, down does the highway go, but at its
destination, you're sure to find fire and definitely not snow!
It's the narrow path that takes you up to the heavens, but the
highway takes you nowhere but down, down, down, you know.
And just with that alone, I'd take God's
way and surely not the highway.
Yes, the heavens where you'll find the Golden Sidewalk, and on it
the Golden Crown of Glory right next to the Book of Life, alright?
Yeah, that's right, you'll find them all up in Heaven,
where you'll also find our Lord, Jesus Christ.
With that, one more thing must I say, which is
that I ask all to remember and never forget.
Yes, to everyone do I say, remember, remember,
remember, and please never forget.
It's God's Way or the Highway!

***By** Jehovah* THROUGH THE HEART, MIND,
AND LEFT HAND OF ***Kevin Moss***

Enter you in at the straight gate: for wide is the gate, and broad is the way, that leads to destruction, and many there be which go in there at: Because straight is the gate, and narrow is the way, which leads unto life, and few there be that find it.
—MATTHEW 7:13–14

God's Word Will Always Stand!

There's just so many in the world today that
really think they're standing tall.
But I'm afraid I must tell them that they're not; in fact,
instead of standing, a lot of them have truly made a fall.
Now whether they fell from a mountain or
off a wall really doesn't matter,
no, it doesn't matter what they fell from for still did they fall.
I believe that so many this has happened to
because they just couldn't hear.
Now a lot of them couldn't hear for they didn't listen when
God made His call, which can happen to us all, all, and all.
And what's really such a shame is, when
it comes to God our Creator,
so many of we the world just seem not to care.
So I say to them, listen here, all of God's commands are
very, very true and are given to both me and you!
Believe me, you-al, God's word will always stand,
stand, and stand for they're His commands.
You may not like or agree with God's laws and
commands, which is on you if that's your plan.
But Always Remember That God's the First Man!
And believe me, since He's God and all was made
by and for He, His word will always stand.
Yes, it was God who gave life, and to both
me and you He gave it too!
But also remember, even though He gave us life, life is still His.
This do I say to all, all, and all, and I say it to
you all again, again, and again yawl.
So, everyone, please remember, remember, remember,
and never ever forget, but do understand.
Yes, let us all understand that God's Word Today, Tomorrow,
just as Yesterday, will always Stand, Stand, and Stand.

By Jehovah THROUGH THE HEART, MIND, AND LEFT HAND OF ***Kevin Moss***

The Lord, kills, and makes alive: He brings down to the grave, and brings up. The Lord makes poor, and makes rich: He brings low and lifts up. He raises up the poor out of the dust, and lifts up the beggar from the dunghill, to set them among princes, and to make them inherit the Throne of Glory: for the pillars of the Earth are the Lord's, and He has set the world upon them.

—1 SAMUEL 2:6–8

My Feet Stand on His

God gave everything; He made a gift!
Yes, a gift of some kind He gave all of we, for He makes
nothing for nothing and nothing with nothing.
And believe me, the gift He's given you is yours as the gift He's
given me is mine, but we're first to be His at all times. Now I
would like to use the gift He's given me for I know, through
its power, I would be able to stand on my own two feet. Yes, I
would be able to stand straight up with ease on my own two feet
for I would first be standing His, yes, on God's feet, that is.
BELIEVE ME, MY FEET STANDS ON HIS!
Now when you step on one's toe, whosever toe it was you may
have stepped on, you best believe it was God's toe you first hurt.
For once said by God to all of we was "What You Do Unto Him
You Do Unto Me," so believe me, you best make your plea!
And just in case you don't, through God, I'll tell you the reason
why what you didn't see is true and real and will always be.
It's because God Himself is inside of all of we.
Yes, He's inside of you, and He's also inside of me;
yes, He's inside of all of we truly; truly is He.
So please believe me when I say this, for it's coming from the
bottom of my heart that it's so true, yes, it truly, truly is!
Yes, So True It Is, So Believe Me When I Say my Feet Stands on His!
Today I know it's so hard out here in the world,
yes, it is, it is, it is. I truly know it is!
So pick up your cross and follow He, and with the strength you'll
have, I'm sure, you'll see it has been given to you by no one but
He. So stand strong and walk for what is right and not wrong, and
know in your heart that close to the last days isn't very far away,
okay? Now walk, walk, walk straight knowing and saying with faith
so true it truly is that I'm filled with Love, Love, and more Love.
Also Say with Faith, True It Truly Is That My Feet Stand on His and
I Know with the Same Faith My Feet Will Always Stand on His!

By Jehovah THROUGH THE HEART, MIND, AND LEFT HAND OF ***Kevin Moss***

And Jesus knew their thoughts, and said unto them, every kingdom divided against itself is brought to desolation; and every city or house divided against itself shall not stand: And if Satan cast out Satan, he is divided against himself; how shall then his kingdom stand?

—MATTHEW 12:25–26

I Chose You

I chose you, yes, I chose you when you were
just an egg in your mother's womb.
Yes, I did choose you, so you are Mine, true?
Now those words did God once say to me, and believe
me, they've really carried me a long, long ways.
As I know they've carried you, when to you, He also said them too.
Yes, such strong beautiful and powerful
words did He truly say to we.
And we know those words have carried us up so many mountains
and have also safely brought us down so many hills.
They've also guided us across many, many rivers, as they've
protected us in so many dangerous valleys and woods.
So God does say "*I Chose You*" for as He could,
He should for all glory and praise is His!
For instance, sometimes resisting some of Satan's temptations
in life can be as hard as climbing up a mountain.
And other times, desiring some of this world's goodies instead of
accepting God's sweet Love can be as easy as rolling down a hill.
And it seems in this world today going the wrong way can be
as easy as sliding on ice, which is now a frozen river, right?
But we can make it through He, no matter how dangerous
the valley is or how scary the woods may be!
Yes, we can make it through He, for He is Jesus Christ,
and plus, what God said to us is so very, very true.
Yes, Again Does He Say to Us All, "I Chose You.
and Also You, You, and You Too!"

By *Jehovah* THROUGH THE HEART, MIND,
AND LEFT HAND OF ***Kevin Moss***

And he said, The God of our fathers has chosen you, that you should know His will, and see that just One, and should hear the voice of His mouth.

—ACTS 22:14

I Know It Was the Blood

I remember when my life was just oh so down!
I also remember when God lifted it up, and
for me He made it safe and sound.
Believe me, I do remember, for that was when
with Love He turned my life around.
Yes, that He did with Love, Love, and more Love, and
from the bottom of my heart, this I truly know.
Yes, I Know, I Know, I Know; I Know It Was the Blood!
Believe me, it was the blood that gave us
back our lives that we so surely lost.
Yes, it was by the Blood of Jesus Christ that truly paid the cost.
And it cost Jesus His life to truly pay the price
He paid for us all with pure, pure, Love.
So I say this with all my heart, yes, with all my heart
and the same exact Love do I truly say, I know.
Yes, I Know, I Know, I Know It Was the Blood!

***By** Jehovah* THROUGH THE HEART, MIND,
AND LEFT HAND OF ***Kevin Moss***

For Christ also has once suffered for sins, the just for the unjust, that He might bring us to God, being put to death in the flesh, but quickened by the Spirit:

—1 PETER 3:18

Pick up Your Cross and Follow Me

It's time, it's time, yes, it's time; in fact, it's way overdue.
Yes, it's way over due that we all pick up
our cross and begin to follow He.
For to get to heaven besides following He, there is no other way.
And on top of that, in the name of His Father
did not He once say to all of we?
Yes, He said to all of we the world!
"Pick Up Your Cross and Follow Me!"
The point here is, we all need Jesus Christ in our lives
just to get that lift that we can only get from He.
Jesus Christ, the First Son of God, is the only one
that can lift us up to the heavens high.
Do not you see?
And it's also true that He, our Lord and Savior,
Jesus Christ, is both the Lift and the Key.
Now may we all hold this in our heart forevermore for
this is the way it is to be, and truly that's for sure.
Remember, Jesus did say that phrase to all of we
one time, and this phrase I once again repeat.
Yes, He said to all the world.
"Pick Up Your Cross and Follow Me!"
Now it was He that made those footprints in the dirt
up that narrow path and left them all for us to see.
So believe me, it's time those prints that He so surely left, we all
begin to follow up that narrow path, that we may be with He.
So I say out loud to all the world that again it's to be, yes, it is to be
as Christ clearly said to we all the world, yes, to both you and me.
YES, HE SO CLEARLY SAID TO ALL OF WE THE WORLD,
"Pick Up Your Cross and Follow Me!"

***By** Jehovah* THROUGH THE HEART, MIND,
AND LEFT HAND OF ***Kevin Moss***

All scripture is given by inspiration of God, and is profitable for doctrine, for reproof, for correction, for instruction in righteousness.

—2 TIMOTHY 3:16

The Ten Commandments

And God spoke all these words, saying, "*I am the Lord, thy God who has brought thee out of the land of Egypt out of the house of bondage.*"

1. *Thou shalt have no other gods before Me, Thou shalt not make unto thee any graven image or any likeness of anything that is in heaven above or the earth beneath or the water under the earth.*

(Believe Me, Trying to Duplicate God Is
Surely Nothing but a Course.)

2. *Thou shalt not bow thyself down to them nor serve them for I, the Lord, thy God, am a jealous God, visiting the iniquity of the fathers upon the children of the third and fourth generation of them that hate Me: showing mercy unto thousands of them that Love Me and keep My commandments.*

(With That Do I Say May We All Keep His Commands,
for It's God's Word That Shall Always Stand.)

3. *Thou shalt not take the name of thy Lord thy God in vain for the Lord will not hold him guiltless that taketh His name in vain.*

(So Don't Ever Swear, Which Is Taking God's
Name in Vain, Don't Swear upon Anything,
His Throne, Footstool, nor the Hair on Your Head
or the Home of Jesus Christ, He Said.)

4. *Remember the Sabbath day, to keep it holy, six days shalt thy labor and do all thy work.*

But the seventh day is the Sabbath of the Lord, thy God: in it thou shalt not do any work, thou, nor thy son, nor thy daughter, thy manservant, nor thy maidservant, nor thy cattle, nor thy stranger that is within thy gates: For in six days the Lord made the Heaven, the Earth and Sea and all that in them is, and rested on the seventh day: Where for the Lord blessed the Sabbath day and hollowed it.

(So on the Holy Day Are We to Rest Our Hearts, Minds,
Bodies, and Souls, in Whole, Which Includes Our
Family's, Cattle, and the Strangers Within Our Gate.)
"NOW ISN'T THAT JUST GREAT?"

5. *Honor thy Father and thy Mother: that thy days may be long upon the land which the Lord thy God giveth thee.*
(Yes, We Must Honor Them for She's the Mother but God's the Father and of Both We Only Get One.)
6. *Thou shalt not kill.* 7. *Thou shalt not commit adultery.* 8. *Thou shalt not steal.* 9. *Thou shalt not bear false witness against thy neighbor.* 10. *Thou shalt not covet thy neighbor's house, thy shalt not covet thy neighbor's wife, nor his manservant, nor his maidservant, nor his Ox, nor his Ass, nor anything that is thy neighbor's.*

By Jehovah THROUGH THE HEART, MIND, AND LEFT HAND OF ***Kevin Moss***

And this is His commandment, that we should believe on the name of His Son Jesus Christ, and love one another, as He gave us commandment.

—1 JOHN 3:23

Know I'm at the Door

A little ways back, the First Son of God, yes, Jesus
Christ, who's the Bright Shining Light,
did shine His light on we the world when He said,
"When you see these signs, know I'm at the door!"
But it seems a lot of people in the world today still have no sight!
Take a look around you and tell me, what do you see?
I'd say just a crazy, mixed-up world if you asked me!
At the time it seems America is still trying to find a way
to escape the eclipse by finding a way to live in space.
And while we're here on earth, ISIS is still trying to kill all
of we, which will wipe the smile off everyone's face.
But they won't accomplish this goal for we're already
seeing the signs that Jesus Christ said that when these
signs we did see, we are to know that He's at the door.
Yes, that's what He said, believe me.
And so many signs are being seen today, like all the earthquakes,
tornadoes, and floods that we're now seeing everyday, okay?
And how about it being sixty degrees in January and twenty
in the month of May? That's unreal as the Coronavirus, I
must say. And with that thought, remember, Jesus Christ did
say it to us all, all and all, meaning the rich and the poor.
Yes, He Surely Did Say.
When You See These Signs, Know I'm at the Door!

***By** Jehovah* THROUGH THE HEART, MIND,
AND LEFT HAND OF ***Kevin Moss***

And you shall hear of wars and rumors of wars: see that you be not troubled: for all these things must come to pass, but the end is not yet. For nation shall rise against nation, and kingdom against kingdom: and there shall be famines, and pestilences, and earthquakes, in divers places. All these are the beginning of sorrows.

—MATTHEW 24:6–8

You Can Play Games or You Can Gain Life

In this life we live today, it seems a lot of people think that the
life they're living is nothing but a game. And on top of that, in
this game they think they're playing, most of them also think
just having money is their best gain. Like when Philadelphia
won the Super Bowl, it seemed like they thought they won life!
But they won nothing but a game, am not I right?
Believe Me, You Can Play Games or You Can Gain Life.
The Choice Is Yours for It's You Who Pays the Price.
Now as I just said, you can play games or you can gain life,
but the only way to gain it is through the blood of Jesus
Christ. For He's the Saving Messiah, who's also the Savior of
we the world, and you can't buy His Blood with money.
For money just can't pay the price!
Which is because He gave His Life to us all when He died
on the Cross; He did it with and for nothing but Love, so
Love is the cost! And that means to be washed clean by the
Blood of Christ, it takes Love, Love, and more Love.
For did He not pay the exact same price with His Own Life?
So You Can Play Games if You Like, or You Can Gain Life.
Again the Choice Is Yours, for It's You Who'll Pay the Price!
Let's take the Winter Olympics, a worldly event that's filled
with game after game. The funny thing about the Olympics
is how it hurts knowing a lot of the world take these games
more serious than they take real life. Yes, most of them take
the pain that they see running through another knowing how
it must hurt as it were one of their Olympian Opponents with
them playing in the snow or just sliding on ice, you know?
So I Once Again Say You Can Play Games or You Can Gain
Life, Yes, You Can, and Remember, the Choice Is Yours.
But Don't Ever Forget It's Also You Who'll Pay the Price!

***By** Jehovah* THROUGH THE HEART, MIND,
AND LEFT HAND OF ***Kevin Moss***

Know ye not that they which run in a race run all, but one receives the prize? So run, that you may obtain. And every man who strives for the mastery is temperate in all things. Now they do it to obtain a corruptible crown; but we an incorruptible. I therefore so run, not as uncertainly; so fight I, not as one who beats the air: But I keep under my body, and bring it into subjection: lest that by any means, when I have preached to others, *I myself should be a castaway.*

—1 CORINTHIANS 9:24–27

Being on the Winning Team

In life I think we'd all like to be on the winning team, you know?
But today we find so many leaving life
losing, and why? I just don't know.
But I know they would have won if they'd just humbled themselves
by picking up their cross and following our Lord, Jesus Christ.
Yes, really if they'd just picked up their cross and
followed Jesus Christ, He who paid the price,
their lives would have been oh so nice.
For believe me, you can't help but win for He's our Lord and Savior
who paid for our sins; yes, with His Own Life, he paid the price.
Now Jesus Christ always coaches the team exactly the
same, yes, and it was He who won the first game.
Now you know what I mean I hope, and if you
don't, I'm sorry for that's just a shame.
But since you don't know, would you let me explain it all to you so?
Well, first it goes like this; believe me when I
say that there's only one winning team!
Now years ago, Jesus Christ, the coach of the winning team up
on a mountain, won the first game by defeating that beast.
Yes, it was there that He changed the scene in so many lives by
defeating that beast, and with Love He brought back Peace.
Yes, Just for Us He Died on the Cross by Paying the Cost!
Jehovah, true Owner, put Emmanuel in charge
of His team, so let Him change your life scene by
scene, putting you on the Winning Team.
Yes, get down to the green and join the Winning
Team, you know what I mean?
For Believe Me, When You Join the Winning Team, Your
Whole Life Will Change for the Better Just Scene by Scene!

***By** Jehovah* THROUGH THE HEART, MIND,
AND LEFT HAND OF ***Kevin Moss***

I am crucified with Christ: nevertheless I live; yet not I, but Christ lives in me: and the life which I now live in the flesh I live by the faith of the Son of God who loved me, and gave Himself for me.

—GALATIANS 2:20

You've Seen the Lord

It's been said for so long now that no one's seen the Lord.
So I say out loud to everyone, think about it, will
you? And then ask yourself, am I sure?
No, you're not sure for what's been said for so long
now is just another lie and also a bore.
Believe me, it is for it's so true, yes, so true it
truly is that we've all seen the Lord!
Again believe me, because we have, for in any way you've
seen Love, old sweet, sweet Love and nothing more.
You've Also Seen the Lord, Once Again Believe
Me, for Truly That's for Sure!
As the love we have for the sun that shines so bright, and the
moon with all the beautiful stars that shine in the night.
How about all the lovely flowers that we all just love to see, as well
as all the lovely, lovely leaves that fall from all the beautiful trees?
For all was made for us by Love, with Love,
and for Love, do not you see?
Yes, it's so true that in any way you've seen Love, oh sweet, sweet
Love, who showed Himself to both you and me with Love.
So You Have Also Seen the Lord from High Up Above!
As all the love that he has for she, and she
for he, he for you and you for me.
For it's really God that's Love and He will always be!
So once again it's really, really true that in any way you've
seen Love, old sweet, sweet Love and nothing more.
Believe Me, You Have Seen the Lord and Truly That's for Sure!

***By** Jehovah* THROUGH THE HEART, MIND,
AND LEFT HAND OF ***Kevin Moss***

Behold, a virgin shall be with a Child, and shall bring forth a Son, and they shall call His name Emmanuel, which being interpreted is, God with us.

—MATTHEW 1:23

Up, Up, Up

You know the word *up* is a very powerful and
high, high word, and it's also a blessing.
Yes, it's a blessing and a gift when God wakes you
up in the morning to a fresh new day.
And you know it's just so beautiful looking up at the great blue
sky in the morning as the sun shines oh so bright and oh so high.
Yes, it shines down its shiny bright rays on those
special mornings as the birds fly by.
But then it's just as exciting looking up to the sky in the night!
Yes, looking up at all the different shapes and sizes that
the moon makes as it and the stars shine so bright.
Amazingly, the clouds make designs of their own
and every day a new picture is drawn.
Now God's the true Artist who sits up high above
the sky looking down at His earthly ground.
And all praise and glory does and should go up to He,
for He's the creator of everything of life that we see.
For was it not He that created every
mountain, flower, bush, and tree?
Yes, it was God that created the birds that fly in the
sky as well as the fish that swim in the sea.
And may we never forget that it was also
He who created both you and me.
So please let us all keep our hearts and minds
up, up, up, yes, up to the sky.
Yes, up to the sky, thanking God continuously
for all His beauty as the wind blows by.
And as the wind blows, I say to *Jehovah* in such a
soft, sweet way; in fact to Him we all should say in
the beginning and at the end of every day.
Yes, every day we should all say up to God, our Heavenly Father
and Creator, again, again, and again, yes, up to Him let us all say,

We Thank You, Our Heavenly Father, for
Another New Day; Yes, up, up, up
to He we all should Pray.

By *Jehovah* THROUGH THE HEART, MIND AND LEFT-HAND OF ***Kevin Moss***

Humility

Submit yourselves therefore to God resist the Devil, and he will flee from you. draw near to God, and He will draw near to you. cleanse your hands, you sinners; and purify your hearts, you double minded. Be afflicted, and mourn, and weep: let your laughter be turned to mourning, and your joy to heaviness. Humble yourselves in the sight of the Lord, and He shall lift you up.

—JAMES 4:7–10

He Vibrates In My Heart And Circles In My Mind!

God truly is Love, and His Love just means the world to me.
That's God the Father, God the Son, and God the Holy
Ghost, three different names belonging to One.
For nothing but Love is the Father, the
Holy Ghost, and also the Son.
Believe me, no matter what form God may be in,
still He's only One, again, again, and again.
Do not you see that it was Love, Love, and more Love that first gave
life to all of we, and then with the same Love He truly set us free!
And that's the Love of God the Father, God the Son, and God
the Holy Ghost, Three that equals One, do not you see?
Now over, over, and over His Love Vibrates in my Heart and round,
round, and round that same Love Circles in the Mind of me.
See Love's a very powerful force; in fact Love's the powerful east
force we have on earth for Love's truly God with a great big burst.
Believe me, God is the Power, and He's also the
Key for as He's in heaven with all His Angels,
He's also here on earth with you and me.
Yes, He really is, and that's how we so easily feel His Vibrations of
Love and with the same Love does He Circle around all of we.
Believe me, for, yes, with Love, Love, and more
Love, He's truly here on earth with all of we, now
tell me with Love, that this you do see?
For truly He Mr. Love, Love, and more Love with all His
Love does Vibrate in my Heart and Circles in my mind.
And really the vibrations I've gotten from His Love deep down
inside my heart has felt so good to me from the very start!
And at the exact same time, His Love also circles round and round
my mind, which makes me feel so good like I'm on a natural high!
THAT'S HOW I FEEL WHEN HE VIBRATES
IN MY HEART AND CIRCLES IN MY MIND
WITH A BIG AMEN JUST ALL THE TIME.

By Jehovah THROUGH THE HEART, MIND, AND LEFT HAND OF ***Kevin Moss***

All things are delivered unto Me of My Father: and no man knows the Son, but the Father; neither knows any man the Father, save the Son, and he to whomsoever the Son will reveal Him.

—MATTHEW 11:27

Only the Love of Father Can Fill the Hole Left by Mother!

When a loving mother is removed from life, an
empty hole is left in one's Heart, right?
Now this hole can only be filled by the Love of *the True Father of Life* who's also the Father of our Lord, Jesus Christ.
But such a big hole can be left in one's heart the day their
mother leaves this life and they truly have to part.
Yes, on that day, a hole does appear in your Heart,
a hole that's oh so big and oh so dark.
Believe me, there's really only one other that
Loves you even more than your mother.
And that's God, the Father who truly Loves us
all, yes, all my sisters and brothers.
And only the Love of He, the True and Only Father, can fill
that empty hole that's left by the loss of one's mother.
And that means, if you don't have God, the Father in
your life, by the blood of Jesus Christ on the day your
mother passes away, you'll probably also have that same
empty hole left in your heart too, I truly must say!
Yes, a big black hole will be left inside of you if you don't have
God, the Father that Loves us even more than our mothers do.
So, all my sisters and brothers, I now end coming
from the Heart just as I did from the start.
Yes, by Saying that Only the Love Of Father
Can Fill That Hole Left by Mother!

***By** Jehovah* THROUGH THE HEART, MIND,
AND LEFT HAND OF ***Kevin Moss***

My son, listen to the instructions of your Father and forsake not the law of your mother: for they shall be an ornament of grace unto your head, and chains about your neck.

—PROVERBS 1:8–9

Honor your Father and Mother: that your days may be long upon the land which the Lord thy God gives you.

—EXODUS 20:12

Who Said a Male Can't Cry?

Tears are drops of a liquid that sometimes fall from our eyes.
And whether their falling because of pain or joy, they'll
still just roll down our face every time we cry.
Now we all have times in our lives where there's days we're
just oh so happy and others when we're just sad, sad, sad.
And then there's times we're just oh so angry and times
when we're happy, happy, happy, just glad, glad, glad.
And believe me, that's because once again tears are just dripping
drops of water that can fall from our eyes when we're happy or sad.
For tears are from our emotions, yes, our feelings
and at times they're just oh so sharp.
Yes, at times they can be just as sharp as a
knife cutting straight down our heart.
Now we all have a heart, and we all have emotions,
yes, feelings that we hold in our heart.
For that's how we carry our feelings in life, and here
we've carried our feelings from the very start.
Now sometimes our feelings comfort us, but
other times they do make us cry.
Now believe me, for I'm sure you know at times how it
really hurts when those tears are falling from our eyes.
For That Alone I Ask All the World, so Someone
Tell Me, Who Said a Male Can't Cry?
I mean, isn't the Male put through the same process
as the Female when brought into the world?
For doesn't the Doctor also spank his bottom, bringing tears to his
eyes at the same time God is filling him with the Breath of Life?
Sure he does, for he, just like she, also holds love for
others deep down inside his heart, alright?
You know the kind of love one has for their
Mother, Father, and Sisters and Brothers.
And just by losing a friend that one dearly, dearly loves
hurts so bad inside that it may bring tears to your eyes.

Yes, once again making you cry, that's right, just as one cries tears of
pain when spanked on the bottom for doing wrong and not right.
Again tears may fall from your eyes, and, yes, I'm sure
they'll be tears of joy falling from so many eyes when
we see King Jesus Christ on that special, special day
coming through the clouds high up in the sky!

***By** Jehovah* THROUGH THE HEART, MIND,
AND LEFT HAND OF ***Kevin Moss***

And he lifted up his eyes, and saw his brother Benjamin, his mother's son, and said, is this your younger brother, of whom you spoke unto me? And he said, God be gracious unto you, my son. And Joseph made haste; for his bowels did yearn upon his brother: and he sought where to weep; and he entered into his chamber, and wept there.
—GENESIS 43:29–30

Looks Fake but It's Real!

Man once looked fake and just so unreal.
Really, he did when he was just a model in
the dirt laying there oh so still.
But under God's will, he was then made whole and oh so real.
Yes, he was then made whole when God blew the
Breath of Life in him and he became a living soul.
Looks Fake, but It's Real, Just Oh So Real!
I thought it was said that movies were fake!
As it was also said that whether you're looking
at a movie in a Theater or home on your set, the
people you're looking at are just Actors.
But we the people looking at them are real, plus what we're seeing
in the movies is really happening in our world, would not you say?
Looks Fake, But It's Real, Just Oh So Real!
There's so many today that don't believe that God's not a fairy tale,
but He's Love, Love, and more Love that's oh so real and true.
And there's just as many that don't believe or accept that God's
the One that will see you through, through, and through.
And what you see around you happening every single day, believe,
because you too play a part in this movie called life, Okay?
Now this is a movie that God wrote a long time
ago, but the way man acts today makes the show
look like it's not very nice, you know?
But Jesus Christ, yes, God is truly the Director and also the Star
of the whole show who will soon be coming back to get us!
BUT ARE YOU READY TO GO?

***By** Jehovah* THROUGH THE HEART, MIND,
AND LEFT HAND OF ***Kevin Moss***

And the Lord God formed man of the dust of the ground, and breathed into his nostrils the breath of life; and man became a living soul.

—GENESIS 2:7

For we brought nothing into this world, and it is certain that we can carry nothing out.

—1 TIMOTHY 6:7

IT MAY SOUND FAKE, BUT BELIEVE ME, IT'S REAL, JUST OH SO REAL!

But Love Is!

Evil's not good, nor is it right.
It hurts just like pain, so why do we fight?
You should show lovingkindness every day and night.
Because wrong makes you weak, for strong it's just not.
BUT LOVE IS!

Problems put worry on our hearts and minds
with a great big buzz all the time.
And in every way, it hurts both him and her, and that's not kind.
It's funny though for it seems a lot of times when we have
these kind of feelings, it always feels like no one's there.
Yes, it seems like no one's there to help us out
by showing that they really do care.
BUT LOVE IS!

Love helps you up and then gently sets you down.
Love puts a smile on your face as it removes that ugly frown.
Plus Love will wipe away your every tear and at
the very same time remove all your fear.
Sometimes we feel just so alone and believe in our hearts
that we have no one for us that really, really cares.
But Love's Here!
For God Is Love, Love, and More Love, and Yes, He Truly,
Truly Cares, and Believe Me, He'll Always Be Here.

***By** Jehovah* THROUGH THE HEART, MIND,
AND LEFT HAND OF ***Kevin Moss***

But the hour comes, and now is, when the true worshippers shall worship the Father in spirit and in truth: for the Father seeketh such to worship Him. God is a Spirit: and they who worship Him must worship Him in spirit and in truth.

—JOHN 4:23–24

The Moon, the Stars, and You!

When the moon and stars come out at night, it
is then that I love to squeeze you tight.
To kiss your lips while looking in your ebony eyes that
shine so bright is the kind of dream that I have at night.
But even though the day has surely come to an end
and sleep has closed my eyes once again.
I still only see you in my dreams.
Yes, I only see you in my dreams as I rest my head in the moonlight.
Now you can best believe that at this time of the
night, I'm making my wish on a star.
And also that the wish I make is that your
love for me never goes far.
Believe me, my Love, I pray to have you in my arms tonight oh so
tight as I drift off to sleep under the stars and the bright moonlight.

***By** Jehovah* THROUGH THE HEART, MIND,
AND LEFT HAND OF ***Kevin Moss***

And The Lord God caused a deep, sleep to fall upon Adam, and he slept: and He took one of his ribs, and closed up the flesh instead thereof; And the rib, which the Lord God had taken from man, made He woman, and brought her unto the man. and Adam said, this is now bone of my bones and flesh of my flesh:

She shall be called Woman, because she was taken out of Man.

—GENESIS 2:21–23

If a man also lie with mankind, as he lieth with a woman, both of them have committed an abomination: they shall surely be put to death; their blood shall be upon them.

—LEVITICUS 20:13

Two Wrongs Doesn't Make a Right!

Some things people do to others today just hurts
so bad, and it's wrong and surly not right!
And to wrong them back as they've wronged you
isn't right either; plus it's dark, not bright!
So please do as our Lord Jesus Christ said we're
supposed to and turn the other cheek, would you?
Now there's so many today that believe that this
is what turning the other cheek means.
To them, it means if one hits you on your left side, you're
to turn and let them hit you on your right side.
But that's only part of what you're to do, and that's only if you have
to, but what it means you're to do is be the bigger one, I must say.
Yes, you're to be the bigger one by ignoring
the other and just walking away.
You remember what Mom always told you almost every
single day, come on, you remember what she'd always say.
Yes, she'd say two wrongs doesn't make a right, and
no, it doesn't in any way you put it, Okay?
Now we must all face the fact that as it was then, it
still is today for once again it's right, I must say.
Yes, it is for as blind is still blind and sight is still sight in the
exact same way wrong is still wrong and right is still right.
So please, everyone, don't do what's wrong, do what's right,
by just picking up your cross and following Jesus Christ.
Yes, Jesus Christ, who is the Saving Messiah for it's He who's the
Savior of Life and it's also He who makes one's day oh so bright!
Believe me, wrong, wrong, wrong we just shouldn't do, nor
do, do, or do, which goes for us all, yes, both me and you.
Love, Love, and More Love Is Nothing but Right and
God's Both, Yes, Love, and the Bright Shining Light.

***By** Jehovah* THROUGH THE HEART, MIND,
AND LEFT HAND OF ***Kevin Moss***

Then the soldiers of the governor took Jesus into the common hall, and gathered unto Him the whole band of soldiers, and they stripped Him, and put on Him a scarlet robe, and when they had platted a crown of thorns, they put it upon His head, and a reed in His right hand: and mocked Him, saying, hail, King of the jews! And they spit upon Him, and took the reed, and smote Him on the head, and after that they had mocked Him, they took the robe off from Him, and put His own raiment on Him, and led Him away to crucify Him.

—MATTHEW 27:27–31

Beginning to End, End to Beginning

Dark, dark, dark shall the end truly be!
Yes, it will, but the New Beginning will be oh so bright
for God will be both the Heaven and the Light.
On top of that, forevermore He'll be all the light
we'll ever need in the day and in the night.
And today it feels like we're so close to the
end, followed by the New Beginning.
Alright, alright, alright?
Believe me, for today we're in, yes, in the last days,
and it seems so dark in this evil world we live in.
And it's just a shame that so many will lose and surely not win.
But for all those washed clean by the blood of Christ, it shall be a
new beginning for them all, all and all, and surely not the end.
On top of that, for them, it will be the beginning of walking
a pond, the Golden Sidewalk of the new Heaven Earth.
Which will be when Love, Love, and more
Love will nothing else but burst.
For no more will there be evil, hurt, or pain; no,
they'll never exist again, no, not ever, so believe
me for, yes, they've truly come to an end.
Yes, those kind of feelings will finally be over, all my sisters and
brothers, and Happiness, Peace, and Joy will truly take over.
Now may all remember that Bright, Bright,
Bright shall the New Beginning be.
So give your life back to God through Jesus Christ
for that's how it will be; again believe me, for it
will be this way, just watch, and you'll see!
Yes, You Shall See the New Beginning, Beginning,
and Beginning over and over Again.

***By** Jehovah* THROUGH THE HEART, MIND,
AND LEFT HAND OF ***Kevin Moss***

But the day of the Lord will come as a thief in the night; in the which the Heavens shall pass away with a great noise, and the elements shall melt with a fervent heat, the earth also and the works that are therein shall be burned up.

—2 PETER 3:10

You Can't Judge a Book by the Cover!

You can't judge a book by the cover, and that
goes for me, he, she, and all others.
For if you try to judge a book from the outside, you'll
never know the true story of the book on the inside.
Why not? For aren't all stories of a book on the inside?
Everyone should know that the story is on the inside
from the start, for on the inside is where you find
THE BRAIN, MIND, SOUL, and the HEART!
Yes, this is where we find the true story of all,
no matter how short, skinny, fat, or tall.
Now I've come to learn that some of the most prettiest
and loveliest people you ever saw on the outside
also come to be some of the most selfish, nastiest,
and ugliest people on the inside.
Now remember, it's on the inside you find the true color of all.
The funny thing is, when you turn your head,
heart, and mind back around again.
You also come to see that others may not look as fine on the outside;
But they still come to be some of the most Nicest,
Sweetest, kindest, and best of friends.
And that's why you must never judge a book
from the cover, no, don't do that!
Because first of all, it's one of the most biggest of
sins, and that's because our Creator did say.
And please remember He said it, not me, yes,
it one day to Samuel the Lord did say.

***By** Jehovah* THROUGH THE HEART, MIND,
AND LEFT HAND OF ***Kevin Moss***

The LORD said unto Samuel, Look not on his countenance, or the height of his stature; because I have refused him: for the Lord sees not as a man sees; for man looks on the outward appearance, but the LORD looks at his heart.

—1 SAMUEL 16:7

Their Truly One, One, One!

Truly, truly, truly it's so true that they're truly *One*, that's God the
Father, God the Holy Ghost, and Jesus Christ, God the Son.
But we still have those in the world today that still don't
believe and ask the question of how, why, and when.
The answer is that God, our Heavenly Father, has so much
Love for all of we such an evil world; yes, He really does.
That He sent His Son, *Emmanuel,* in another form of
Himself from His heavens high down to His earth below.
Yes, He did, just to rescue us, you know? And He did rescue
them that believed in Him, and He plus showed us the way.
So if there's anyone, or day, to remember it's truly Jesus
Christ and the day He died on the cross for us.
Now that was the day they nailed Him to a cross when He
rescued us, and I'm sure it truly hurt, but still it was a plus.
So truly that's a day for us all to know, remember,
believe, and also truly accept and surely not forget!
For on that day He gave His life for our sins by
paying the wage of sin for us all, yes, DEATH!
Now once you believe, accept, and repent to God through
Jesus Christ right then and there, Jesus becomes your Savior.
For again He paid that wage for us all, so by His blood,
we were washed clean of our sins with pure, pure love.
Now Tell Me Truly, Truly, Truly Wasn't That a Win, and Now Do
You See How Much They're truly ***One*** again, again, and again?
That's God the Father, God the Son, and God the
Holy Ghost, the Three That Equals ***ONE***!
Yes, here we have three different forms of God equaling only one.
Now from All These Straight Words I've Shared Here with
You Today, Just Tell Me You Don't Get It in Any Way.
And if there's anyone that doesn't get it, then it goes like so, Okay?
Oh You Great *Jehovah* Are Surely Number ***One***, and, Jesus
Christ, Truly You're the Savior of Life and You're the Only ***One***!
And Let Us Not Forget About the Holy Spirit,

Yes, the Comforter Who's Truly the ***One*** and Only Holy Ghost and Truly Number ***One.*** So ***one*** + ***one*** + ***one*** still = ***ONE*** for the Father, Son, and Holy Ghost are three different forms of God that's truly only ***One***!

By *Jehovah* THROUGH THE HEART, MIND, AND LEFT HAND OF ***Kevin Moss***

But while he thought on these things, behold, the Angel of the Lord appeared unto him in a dream, saying, Joseph, thou son of David, fear not to take unto you Mary thy wife: for that which is conceived in her is of the Holy Spirit.

—MATTHEW 1:20

Jesus said unto him, Have I been so long with you, and yet have you not known Me Philip? He that has seen Me has seen the Father; and how do you say then, Show us the Father? Do you believe not that I am in the Father, and the Father in Me? The words that I speak unto you I speak not Myself: but the Father who dwells in Me, He does the works.

—JOHN 14:9–10

Eternally Burn!

You old cruel, cruel world, tell me, tell me, please tell me, will you
ever learn that if you're not washed clean by the Blood of Christ
You Shall Eternally Burn?
Eternal is one of the biggest and longest words I've ever heard.
Yes, long eternally is for eternally means forever.
That's right, eternally is forever, which
means for ever, ever, and ever.
So being washed clean by the blood of Christ is
something we must do to receive Eternal Life.
Now I pray you the world, yes, pray that you all listen, hear, and
learn for if you don't, where you're going, you shall Eternally Bum!
Now there's only one way to the Father, and truly that's the Son.
Yes, the first Son of God who's the Saving Messiah, and His
name is Jesus Christ, yes, that's right. And Jesus Christ, like
His Father, is nothing but Love, Love, and more Love, alright.
Believe me, He's just like His Father from high up above.
We're just about at that point now when
we shall all bow down to He.
And believe me, at that point, they'll only be two
things He'll have to say to just all of we.
Now to some, it'll be "Go through, go through, go through,
My child," and to others, it'll be "I do not know you,
so I cast you down!" Now I pray you all believe me and
hope you understand and learn that whoever He casts
down will truly, truly, truly forever, ever, and ever
ETERNALLY BURN, BURN, BURN!

***By** Jehovah* THROUGH THE HEART, MIND,
AND LEFT HAND OF ***Kevin Moss***

But the Day of the Lord will come as a thief in the night; in the which the Heavens shall pass away with a great noise, and the elements shall melt with a fervent heat, the earth also and the works that are therein shall be burned up. Seeing then all these things shall be dissolved, what manner of persons ought ye to be in all Holy conversation and Godliness, looking for and hasting unto the coming of the day of God, wherein the Heavens being on fire shall be dissolved, and the element shall melt with fervent heat? Nevertheless we, according to His promise, look for new Heavens and a new Earth, wherein dwells Righteousness.

—2 PETTER 3:10–13

Your Word Is Your Bind

Your word comes out your mouth, and truly it's your bind!
But it first comes from your heart and also from your mind.
So you must stand by your word or you've just told a lie!
And you must not lie to anyone for everyone is your neighbor.
Now remember God's law is "Thy Shall Not Bear False Witness
Unto Thy Neighbor" for that's lying to your brother.
And we all must follow God's laws—
meaning me, he, she, and all others.
So Always Remember and Never Forget Not to Lie to Anyone!
Now Do You Get It?
Yes, Always Remember, Your Word Is Your Bind!
Yes, it is, and even though it comes out your mouth, it
still first comes from your heart and your mind.

***By** Jehovah* THROUGH THE HEART, MIND,
AND LEFT HAND OF ***Kevin Moss***

And the tongue is a fire, a world of iniquity: so is the tongue among our members, that it defiles the whole body, and set on fire the course of nature; and it is set on fire of Hell.

—JAMES 3:6

The wicked walk on every side, when the vilest men are exalted.

—PSALM 12:8

Another Link in God's Chain

God made it very clear to me that I have nothing to
fear, for I'm truly another link in His chain.
It's so amazing that through God's Love and our Faith in
His Love is like having a Precious, Precious Pearl.
His chain of Love first runs through and from Heaven
down to the Earth and through we His World.
On top of that, He also put so many other human beings
who are spiritually linked to He on His Earth.
And He put we on this Earth to spread His Love and Word,
making some of the Best starting from the worse.
And we His links with His Precious, Precious Love
really do make a pretty strong chain, you know?
And it's really so easy to become another link in God's
chain, and it's not a loss but truly is a Gain.
And all you do sincerely from your heart is just repent!
Yes, repent to God through His first Son, our Lord Jesus Christ.
Through He, ask for forgiveness with Love and
you'll become a link in God's chain.
And believe me, when it comes to this
kind of chain, there's only one.
It's also so easy as I said before, yes, just pick up
your cross and begin to follow "HE."
Believe Me, Just as the Father of Love, the Son
Also Says to Us All, "Come, Come, Come!"
(And This Is How We All Come Together!)
1. Admit to yourself that you too are a sinner, which shouldn't
be hard because through the sin of Adam, we all are.
2. With all your heart, say that you do believe that
Jesus Christ is truly the first Son of God, who died
for us all and who can and will save you.

3. And if you believe in your heart what you just
said, that Jesus Christ can and will save you,
Then you just became another link in God's chain.
Now Tell Me That Wasn't Easy, Coming with Nothing Else but
Love, Love, and more Love, which is not a loss but truly is a Win.

***By** Jehovah* THROUGH THE HEART, MIND,
AND LEFT HAND OF ***Kevin Moss***

I tell you, in the night there shall be two men in a bed; the one shall be taken, and the other shall be left. Two women shall be grinding together at a mill; the one shall be taken, and the other left. Two men shall be in a field; the one shall be taken, and the other left. And they answered and said unto Him, Where Lord? And He said unto them, wheresoever the body is, thither will the eagles be gathered.

—LUKE 17:34–37

Pastor Month

October is the tenth month of the year, and *Jehovah*,
our Heavenly Father, has made it Pastor month.
So Pastor Month is a set time of the year to give love,
grace, and thanks to the Pastors of God's temples here.
For believe me, they are the true body parts of the First
Church, yes, Jesus Christ our Savior, alright?
I believe it's such a blessing to have such remarkable Pastors
as some of the Pastors we have today, don't you?
All Pastors who have been chosen by God have been chosen
to spread His Love and Word, haven't you heard?
Pastors as Moses, David, Solomon, Peter, Luke, John,
Paul, Timothy, and James and the best Pastor of all will
always be Jesus Christ in spreading His word!
But let us never forget about the Pastors of today as Rev. Elder
Jones who was a Pastor that was always there and never gone.
And please, let us always remember to keep them
in our prayers, showing them lovingkindness as
God has showed to us all everywhere.
Now may we all show that same kindness and love with
Love, Love, and more Love to them all, all, and all.
And on Top of That, Let Us Show Them Pure Lovingkindness
with Nothing but Love at Their Every Call!
Let everyone remember this month every year, and if you really care
for it as all other holidays, celebrate this one too at least once a year.
Yes, let us celebrate remembering all Pastors, in
our hearts, minds, bodies, and souls.
AND LET US NEVER FORGET PASTOR MONTH
AT ALL, BUT ALWAYS REMEMBER ALL OUR
PASTORS WITH LOVE IN WHOLE!

***By** Jehovah* THROUGH THE HEART, MIND,
AND LEFT HAND OF ***Kevin Moss***

Let a man so account of us, as of the Ministers of Christ and stewards of the mysteries of God.

—1 CORINTHIANS 4:1

A Strong Foundation

A foundation is what we build on.
And believe me, whatever we're building must
have a strong foundation to stand.
Yes, as strong as a rock the foundation must be.
For if it's not built on a foundation that's as strong as a rock,
whatever was built will wash away like sand under God's command.
So please, everyone build your life on God the Father, God
the Son, and God the Holy Ghost, One strong Foundation!
For no matter what the problem was, is, or may come to
be, believe me, Jesus Christ can and will set you free.
He, the first Son of God, will hold you, carry you,
keeping you safe and sound, and in any storm
you may be in, He'll never let you down.
So build your life on God the Father, God the Son,
and God the Holy Ghost by repenting right now
and become another one of God's posts.
Yes, stop for a moment and take a look around, and as myself, you'll
also see so many things man has built today are truly falling down!
And believe me, they're truly falling through a big
black hole where the fire is high and oh so hot.
And on top of that, the fire won't be going out,
and whoever falls in it won't be getting out, but as
my Father said, they shall eternally burn.
Believe me, what God, our Heavenly Father, once
said to me, and you is so very, very true.
Yes, so true it really is that if you're not washed clean by the
blood of Christ, you'll eternally burn, burn, burn and that's
eternally true, and that goes for whoever in that big black hole
fell through, and believe me, that goes for both me and you!
And it goes for all others too just like me and you!
So once again do I say build your life on a strong foundation.
Yes, a foundation by the name of God the Father,
God the Son, and God the Holy Ghost.

Just One Strong Foundation!

By** Jehovah* THROUGH THE HEART, MIND, AND LEFT HAND OF ***Kevin Moss

For No Other Foundation Can No Man Lay Than That Is Already Laid Which Is, *Jesus Christ.*

—1 CORINTHIANS 3:11

We All Come Together, Truly We Are One

We all come together for truly we are one!
And that's because He, the first One and only God, did make man,
and He made man for Himself from the dust of the ground.
And then from him, He made her, and
then He set the two both down.
He then told the two one He had just made, to be
fruitful, multiply, and make more of yourself.
If you ask me, that means we do come together; yes,
we're one, like one big giant or little, tiny elf.
And that's me, he, she, and everyone else! No, it really doesn't
matter what race, creed, or color you are, for we're all human beings.
And we do come together, if you know what I mean. Yes,
believe me we do come together like one big candy bar!
The problem is that so many in our world today are so sour, just
so sour and also unsweet are most people in our world today
And so many are tired of its hate and no
longer of it do they want to eat!
Now Do You Get the Beat?
Well, the Beat Goes As Just Said, Today Most
People Are Tired of This Worlds Sourness!
And No Longer of It Do They Choose to Eat!
And I guess that's because it seems that in this world today all
you see around you is kill Beat, Kill Beat, and more Kill Beat.
And with our world being this way today, I just
don't understand, accept, and surely don't agree for
racism is wrong, *towards both you and me!*
So as *Jehovah*, yes, God, our Heavenly Father, we too are to
be filled with Love, Love, and more Love, yes, we do, true?
So I must say out loud to everyone that we're truly running
out of time, which means it'll soon be over out and done.
So with Love, let us come together and be that one we surely are
to be; yes, let us all come together with Love, yes, just everyone.

Yes, as God, the Father, Let Us All Hold Out Our Arms Opened Wide with Love and Come Together As ***ONE***!

By** Jehovah* THROUGH THE HEART, MIND, AND LEFT HAND OF ***Kevin Moss

And God blessed them, and God said unto them, Be fruitful, and multiply, and replenish the earth and subdue it: and have dominion over the fish of the sea, and over the fowl of the air, and over every living thing that moves upon the earth.

—GENESIS 1:28

What Happened to Respect?

Respect, Respect, Respect Just what has happened to you?
To me, it seems like you don't exist anymore,
Mr. Respect, is that not true?
But why's that Mr. Respect for you're just
another form of love, aren't you?
I mean, Mr. Respect, without you in the
world, just what are we going to do?
For today all this world seems to know and almost all
it seems to see is disrespect, the opposite of thee.
And that's because a lot of our world today no longer knows the
meaning of love; no, they don't like, they only know hate, you see?
Mr. Respect, you were once one of the sweetest ones in life, I know
you were, for your fist name was and still is Jesus Christ, right?
And remember, Mr. Respect, it was through
you that so many saw the Light!
It was also through you that the Light they saw, they saw in the day
and the night, and with respect, I ask the world, isn't that right?
Now one more time do I ask you, Mr. Respect, and I know
that you'll tell me with respect, nothing but the truth.
So, Mr. Respect, I ask, yes, I ask you again, again, and again,
now please tell me just what has happened to you, my Friend?

***By** Jehovah* THROUGH THE HEART, MIND,
AND LEFT HAND OF ***Kevin Moss***

And God saw that the wickedness of man was great in earth, and that every imagination of the thoughts of his heart was only evil, CONTINUALLY.

—GENESIS 6:5

There's Only One Judge

In this world today, it seems we have so many that
will so easily place their opinion on another.
Now I know how that old saying goes where it was said by so
many people, yes, so many times one would say to another.
(*Opinions Are like Bottoms, for Everybody Has One!*)
Remember now, *everybody* means we all and not just one.
And let's not forget about *JOHN 8:7*, where the
Judge did say, yes, He the Son of God said,
"He That Never Sinned Cast the First Stone!"
Now today I know there's a lot of stones being casted and
there's so many of us casting them on, on, and on.
But I think I need to tell a lot of you today that you best be careful
of the stones you're casting and who you're casting them at.
And that's because there's only one Judge, and believe me, that's a fact.
Now please remember, He's the One who first walked up that
narrow path and left His footprints in the dirt for us all to follow.
You know, the one that didn't put Himself first but put
Himself last, for all we, yes, man, who's just been the worst.
Emmanuel was the name that was first given to He who gave His
life for all, yes, both you and me, when He was nailed to a cross.
Yes, it was Jesus Christ who truly paid the cost, and don't let
anyone tell you different, for believe me, He's the Boss!
And Through Him, Just So Many Have Won, who,
Without Him, Would Surely Have Lost.
Now to you all these things do I say and do I say these things with
Love, Love, and more Love, asking you to believe me, OKAY?
Yes, Believe me, He was the One who came down from the
heavens high above and walked this earth for all of us with Love.
Believe Me Again for There's Only One *JUDGE*, and That
ONE Is And Will Always Be *JESUS CHRIST*, You See?

***By** Jehovah* THROUGH THE HEART, MIND,
AND LEFT HAND OF ***Kevin Moss***

God stands in the congregation of the mighty; He judges among the gods. How long will you judge unjustly, and accept the persons of the wicked? Selah, defend the poor and fatherless: do justice to the afflicted and needy. Deliver the poor and needy: rid them out of the hand of the wicked. They know not, neither will they understand; they walk on in darkness: all the foundations of the earth are out of course.

—PSALM 82:1–8

I Shall Judge All!

There's only one judge, and we should all know who that is.
Yes, I believe everyone should know who the real and true Judge is!
For it's true that He's the only real Judge and
it's also true that everything is His.
And it was all done by God's Love, Mercy, and Grace and with Jesus
Christ, His first Son's Love, Strength, and His Strong, Strong Faith.
Yes, I know with faith He truly Saved my life
and put a great big smile on my face.
And then God the Father said to He, God the Son, all is yours for
you showed nothing but love to Me and all the world when I called.
And just for that alone allows He, God the Son, to say to everyone
whether they're a parent, daughter, or son He did say to everyone,
"*I SHALL JUDGE ALL!*"
Yes, Jesus Christ, who's the Lord of Lords and
King of Kings, shall judge all, all, and all.
Yes, a world that He fairly earned with His true Blood and Life; yes,
with His precious, precious blood He did pay the price, alright?
So let us all thank Him, thank Him, yes, thank Him again, again,
and again because for us all He did stand tall when He was called.
And believe me, just for that alone earned Him the right to say with
so much heart, heart, and more heart and plenty of ball, He did say,
"*ALL SHALL BOW TO ME, AND I SHALL JUDGE ALL!*"

***By** Jehovah* THROUGH THE HEART, MIND,
AND LEFT HAND OF ***Kevin Moss***

Judging Others

Speak not evil one of another, brethren. He who speaks evil of his brother, and judges his brother, speaks evil of the law, and judges the law: but if you judge the law, you are not a doer of the law, but a judge. There is the one Lawgiver, Who is able to save and destroy: who are you who judges another?

—JAMES 4:11–12

Jesus said unto him, I am the Way, the Truth, and the Life: no man comes unto the Father but by Me.

—JOHN 14:6

I Am That I Am

I am the Heavenly Father, I am the Saving Son and
Me, He and the Holy Ghost will always be One.
I created the Heavens, and I created the Earth, yes,
I created the Best, starting from the worst.
For I created all life, meaning Man, Reptile, Foul, Fish, and
Beast; yes, I created the best, and I created the least.
Believe Me, there's not another that can give life
or create man, for I'm the only God.
I Am That I Am!
Yes, it was Me who created the Seas, and I also created
all Mountains, Flowers, Bushes, and Trees.
It was also I who made the Green, Green Grass along
with the Present, Future, as well as the Past.
So again do I tell you, yes, I tell you all again that I'm the only
God, and remember this everyone again, again, and again!
Now let all give praise to Me for do I also
tell you again that truly, truly, truly.
I Am That I Am!
Yes, it's Me, *Jehovah*, that's the Greatest and the Best, but it's not
Me, your Heavenly Father, but you the earthly man that must pass
THE TEST!
Now the test that we must pass is just doing what's right.
Do not you see that, yes, it's God's will that this test we
must pass, and just by passing it, God will Set us free.
And I'll also give you Eternal Life with Happiness,
Peace, and Joy to live eternally.
Now Me being able to set you free, plus all that I've created
for you, Me being God shouldn't be so hard for all to see.
So one more time do I tell you that the Creator of Life I am;
yes, truly, truly I am, and may all remember this forever.
For *I Am That I Am!*

By** Jehovah* THROUGH THE HEART, MIND, AND LEFT HAND OF ***Kevin Moss

The day is yours, the night is also yours: You have prepared the light and the sun. You have set all the borders of the earth: You have made summer and winter.

—PSALM 74:16–17

A Blind Leads Another into a Deep, Deep Hole

You must not follow the blind, for they just can't see.
No, they can't, so don't follow Satan follow Jesus
Christ, who can and will set you free.
Yes, truly as free as a bird you shall come to be; yes,
you shall through Jesus Christ, this don't you see?
So with love, follow the Lord Jesus Christ,
who can and will set you free to be.
And this always remember, yes, remember eternally!
Please remember that a Blind Man Leads
Another into a Deep, Deep Hole!
Believe me, because of doing wrong in a
deep, deep hole you shall surely go.
Through Christ, my eyes have been opened, so believe
me, I can see, so what I'm telling you, I know.
Plus, what I'm telling you is nothing but the truth
with plenty of strength and oh so bold.
YES, THAT A BLIND LEADS ANOTHER
INTO A DEEP, DEEP HOLE!

***By** Jehovah* THROUGH THE HEART, MIND,
AND LEFT HAND OF ***Kevin Moss***

Let them alone: they be blind leaders of the blind.

And if the blind lead the blind, both shall fall in the ditch.

—MATTHEW 15:14

The Trumpet Shall Be Blown

The horn so many use to make others aware.
I guess that's because the horn is like a loud, loud whistle
with such strong vibes that so easily float through the air.
Yes, their vibes are just so, so strong and oh so loud and as they
float through the air they make sure that everyone can hear.
Also in the air Jesus Christ shall soon be coming through the clouds,
with an Angel on both His sides blowing their trumpet oh so loud.
This day shall surely come to be and from all the different signs we
surely do see today tells us that day isn't very far away, if you ask me.
And believe me, with Love, Love, and more Love
God has given us chance after chance!
For He first sent His only begotten Son from His heavens down
to His earth to die for we the world who's truly been His worse.
This means you have no excuse to not accept Jesus Christ, the
One that can and will save you by giving you back eternal life.
Just remember, you-al, this day is to come and it won't be long; no,
it won't be long before it gets here, yawl, so hear me, do you hear?
No, Not Very Long at All Will It Be Before We All
Hear Oh So Loud and Clear with Both Our Ears the
Trumpet Being Blown Just About Everywhere!

***By** Jehovah* THROUGH THE HEART, MIND,
AND LEFT HAND OF ***Kevin Moss***

Now this I say, brethren, that flesh and blood cannot inherit the Kingdom of God; neither does corruption inherit incorruption. Behold, I show you a mystery; we shall not all sleep, but we shall all be changed in a moment, in the twinkling of an eye, at the last trump: for the trumpet shall sound, and the dead shall be raised incorruptible, and we shall be changed. For this corruptible must put on incorruptible, and this mortal shall have put on immortality.

—1 CORINTHIANS 15:50–53

Eternal

A word that will always be fascinating to me is
eternal; remember *always* and *forever*,
does eternal mean.
I first got my fascination from this word the
second time I got into it and not the first.
Believe me, the first time I got into it, I wasn't very
fascinated at all; in fact, I was pretty scared and
got nothing but the chills from it, you-al!
Yes, I really did get the chills from it after reading in the Holy Bible
the true Word of God where I read that I could ETERNALLY burn.
And after knowing I could gave me the chills because it made me
feel like a piece of meat on a grilled fire that would never go out.
But I was later so fascinated by the exact same word, yes,
ETERNAL, when it drifted through my mind a second time.
Yes, it drifted through my mind a second time only
this time I was fascinated by it and not scared!
What fascinated me was God was using the word
eternal again, but instead of Him saying eternally
burn, which scared me the first time.
This time, He said, if saved by being washed clean
by the blood of Christ you shall eternally live in
Happiness, Peace, and Joy, yes, with eternal life.
AND TO ME, IT'S REALLY A FASCINATION
KNOWING YOU'VE BEEN GIVEN ETERNAL
LIFE; YES, IT'S JUST OH SO NICE!

***By** Jehovah* THROUGH THE HEART, MIND,
AND LEFT HAND OF ***Kevin Moss***

For the invisible things of Him from the creation of the world, are clearly seen, being understood by the things that are made, even, His eternal power and Godhead; so that they are without excuse:

—ROMANS 1:20

All Shall Bow to Me

We're truly, truly coming to that point!
Yes, that point where we all shall be in the same joint.
You know that joint, and at that point that
God said one day we all would be.
And at all times He truly does mean everything He says, and He
so truly did say every word from His heart to both you and me.
I mean, didn't He say, yes, He said those most powerful
words to everyone of we, again didn't He say to we?
ALL SHALL BOW TO ME!
And believe me, that day is coming soon; yes, one day
we all shall bow to He, yes, at the foot of God, the Son
Jesus Christ is the One and we all shall bow to He!
Yes, one day we all shall bow down to He,
which includes both you and me.
And shouldn't we all with love be willing to bow
down to He who died for all of we?
Sure we should for He first bowed to we for when
He was nailed to a cross, He died for us all, yes,
both you and me, which makes Him boss!
So it shall be as He said for everyone of we, yes, He
said for us all this is the way it would be. You see?
I Tell You That Everyone of Ye Shall Truly Bow down to Me!

***By** Jehovah* THROUGH THE HEART, MIND,
AND LEFT HAND OF ***Kevin Moss***

For unto us a child is born, unto us a Son is given: and the government shall be upon His shoulders: and His name shall be called Wonderful, Counsellor, The mighty God, The everlasting Father, The Prince of Peace.

—ISAIAH 9:6

Just Another Part of Life

You know to me, people really do look at death the wrong way.
For one, they look at death as the end, but it's the beginning.
Yes, it's the beginning of another part of life.
Now it's another part of life for it's something
we shall all experience in life.
Didn't Jesus Christ, the first Son of God, experience it; yes, He
did, for you and me, but He still experienced it, didn't He?
So Again It's Just Another Part of Life
Believe Me, the Time Has Been Set for Our Birth and Our
Death, Yes, for Them Both the Time Has Been Set!
Now those that have left us before the second arrival
of our Lord Jesus Christ are now resting in peace.
Once again, please believe me for when He does arrive to reclaim
what is His, it shall truly be as He said it would be, when He said,
"You Shall First Meet Me in the Sky. Then Shall You All Bow
Down Before Me and Afterwards I Shall Judge You All!"
Then finally you shall eternally live in Happiness,
Peace, and Joy or you shall eternally burn in Hell.
The choice is yours; yes, it is, just as all the
other choices you make in life are!
"And That's Because Just As Those Choices Are, for the Way
You Choose to Go in life Is Also Just Another Part of Life!"

***By** Jehovah* THROUGH THE HEART, MIND,
AND LEFT HAND OF ***Kevin Moss***

Remember how short my time is: wherefore have you made all men in vain? What man is he who lives, and shall not see death? Shall he deliver his soul from the hand of the grave? Selah.
—PSALM 89:47–48

For all this I considered in my heart even to declare all this, that the righteous, and the wise, and their works, are in the Hand of God: no man knows either love or hatred by all that is before them. All things come alike to all: there is one event to the righteous, and to the wicked; to the good and to the clean, and to the unclean; to him who sacrifices, and to him who sacrifices not: as is the good, so is the sinner; and he who swears, as he who fears an oath. This is an evil among all things that are done under the sun, that there is no event unto all: yes, also the heart of the sons of men is full of evil, and madness is in their heart while they live, and after that they go to the dead.

—ECCLESIASTES 9:1–3

The Table Does Turn

May we all remember that everyone had to first
be carried and delivered before given life.
We then were fed and clothed with love, am not I right?
But it was through Jesus Christ and the strength
of the elders that truly brought us through.
And with the same kind of strength and faith,
they carried us through, shouldn't they now be
carried by us with the same strength too?
THE TABLE DOES TURN.
Everyone should be thankful to God the Father
and Jesus Christ, God's First Son, and also to the
Elders who helped He, the First Son.
Now let's not forget it was God who created us
and then gave us life, but by the wrong done by
Adam, it seemed life was just lost for us.
But Jesus came down; yes, all the way down from heaven He did
come down unto His earth and died for us, which was a plus.
Then those strong, strong elders begin to follow He while carrying
us with their strength, and they've carried us a long, long way.
THE TABLE DOES TURN; YES, THE TABLE DOES TURN!
Now if God allows you to also live a long, long life,
then one day you'll be an elder too, right?
So while we're still young and can, let us help the
elders who helped us; yes, help them by making it a
little more easier for them and not so tough!
For if we help them now, one day when we get to be an elder,
God will make sure there's someone there to help us too, Okay?
"REMEMBER!"
THE TABLE TURNS, THE TABLE TURNS,
YES, THE TABLE DOES TURN!

By *Jehovah* THROUGH THE HEART, MIND, AND LEFT HAND OF ***Kevin Moss***

And as you would that men should do to you, do ye also to them likewise.

—LUKE 6:31

May We Be Lifted Up

It seems His demand does outreach our supply.
This I know with faith and do believe, but the question
I ask is, why? I just don't understand why.
I mean, we all should be sharing our love with
each other, for this is God's plan.
Yes, it's God's plan that we all love all with
Love, Love, and more Love.
Yes, we're to love all just as freely and easy as we
receive His Love from high up above.
So let we the world change our ways so that we're
lifted up and not pushed farther down.
Now God's Love truly does exceed ours,
and it's so much greater in reach.
His Love reaches us all, and that's why He gave
the life of His Son to us all with nothing else but
the same Love, for nothing else but Love.
Yet does His demand for us to do as He and love all like
He really out reaches our supply, but again why?
All should know by now that nurturing time
is just about over, you know?
But still does it stand now just as it did then when
it was first said, "You Reap What You Sow!"
We must try so much harder today to educate the unsaved
on how to supply true nourishment, yes, LOVE!
So let us further the development of foster, which is affording,
giving, and sharing in nurture, yes, once again LOVE!
Yes, by showing parental care to all, for as we love
our own blood, we're to love all blood.
So let we the world with LOVE make the changes
that's so needed to be made in this world so we're
lifted up and not pushed farther down.
With God's love, may we all be lifted up to the
heavens high truly safe and sound.

And not be pushed farther down into that fire
that's truly burning underground!

By *Jehovah* THROUGH THE HEART, MIND,
AND LEFT HAND OF ***Kevin Moss***

A Prayer For God's Favor

Lord, You have been favorable unto Your land: You have brought back the captivity of Jacob. You have forgiven the iniquity of Your people, You have covered all their sin. Selah. You have taken away all Your wrath: You have turned Yourself from fierceness of Your anger. Turn us, O God of our Salvation, and cause Your anger toward us to cease. Will You be angry with us forever? Will You draw out Your anger to all generations? Will You not revive us again: that Your people may rejoice in You? Show us Your mercy, O Lord, and grant us Your salvation. I will hear what God the Lord will speak: for He will speak peace unto His people, and to His Saints: but let them not turn again to folly. Surely His salvation is near them who fear Him; that glory may dwell in our land. Mercy and truth are met together; righteousness and peace have kissed each other. Truth shall spring out of the earth; and righteousness shall look down from Heaven. Yes, the Lord shall give that which is good; and our land shall yield her increase. Righteousness shall go before Him; and shall set us in the way of His steps.

—PSALM 85:1–13

Priority and Order

"Priority" is a big powerful and very important
word, would not you say?
The funny thing is, it seems so many people today
don't know what priority even means.
It seems they don't know the meaning of the word
as one they didn't like or never heard.
Now priority means something like first at rank, pertaining
to something or someone more important than another.
For instance, praising God should be your
first priority in life, alright?
And that's because it's God who's our creator;
yes, it is, for it was God who gave us life.
So Everyone Please Get Your Priorities in Order, Would You?
Order is also another word that's used in so many
different ways, would not you say?
For instance, that just sounds like a nice meal they just ordered,
or how about "Put your self at attention,
Soldier, and that's an order!"
And another one that would be a good one to me is, today this
world just seems so out of order, but does it have to be? Believe
me, this piece of art you're now reading have I truly written after
it was sent down to me from the True Author at the Top and He's
first at rank; remember, it was first He who said we're coming
to the end of time and time doesn't get longer but shorter!
Yes, and I bet that's what He meant when He
said, "When You See These Signs,
KNOW I'M AT THE DOOR!"

***By** Jehovah* THROUGH THE HEART, MIND,
AND LEFT HAND OF ***Kevin Moss***

> Therefore take no thought, saying, what shall we eat? Or what shall we drink? Or, wherewithal shall we be clothed? (For after all these things do the Gentiles seek:) for your Heavenly Father knows that you have need of all these things.
>
> —MATTHEW 6:31–32

A Butterfly Flew in My Window

Once upon a time, I was lying in my bed on a nice spring day.
And I was just hoping that love would finally come my way.
I then, all of a sudden, got up from the bed and
opened the shade and let the sunshine in.
And at that very moment, the window blew
open, being pushed by the wind.
And as I looked up, to my surprise, a beautiful Butterfly flew in.
So I whistled to it for its beauty caught my eye.
Then after it flew into the window, it landed in my hands,
and at that very moment, I knew I had a friend.
Now this Butterfly had brought me a love like I never had before,
and it opened up its heart, showing me there was so much more.
Yes, brought to me was Love, Happiness,
Peace with Joy that is so very pure,
And it told me that I had found my love, and this time I was sure.
Now the Butterfly is my love, and the window is my heart,
and I know we will always be happy for we will never part.
And believe me, my Love, I promise you it will always be this way.
Yes, I know it will my Love for you're truly in my heart, and
you and me, my sweet Butterfly, shall never, ever part!

***By** Jehovah* THROUGH THE HEART, MIND,
AND LEFT HAND OF ***Kevin Moss***

And Jesus, when He was baptized, went up straightway out of the water: and, lo, the Heavens opened

unto Him and He saw the Spirit of God descending like a dove, and lighting upon Him:

And a lo voice from heaven saying,

"This Is My beloved Son, Whom I am well pleased."

—MATTHEW 3:16–17

My Rabbit, Bear, and Cat

What's Up, Doc?
Well, I thought I'd stop by and give you a great big hug and
tell you that I miss you and that you'll always have my Love.
Yes, my son, I really do love you, and I just miss
seeing that lovely smile on your cute little face.
My son, may God always bless you as He first
blessed me with you from the start.
Yes, He did bless me with His loving grace like a shining spark
when He made you my little rabbit and your rabbit hole my heart.
And just how are you doing, my little teddy
bear, yes, you my sweet little cub?
Me, Myself, and I really do miss you a lot and
just can't wait to give you a great big hug.
My son, please always remember, Daddy does love you,
and if I ever lost you, what I'd do, I just don't know.
Now, my son, just promise me that you'll always be my
little teddy bear, yes, the teddy bear of my heart.
And as you promise me, I'll promise you that our
love will be forever and will never ever part.
And on the day you were brought into this world, my sweet,
sweet daughter, you put a scratch straight down my heart.
Believe me, the scratch you left upon me
will never go away, my child.
For believe me, on that day, you and your
mother really drew a spark.
And yes, my little girl, it's you that's the kitten
inside of me, yes, my shining star.
Now I end by saying to all of you, my children, yes, my sweet little
pearls, I'll for ever and ever love you, and you'll always be my world!

***By** Jehovah* THROUGH THE HEART, MIND,
AND LEFT HAND OF ***Kevin Moss***

And the Lord visited Sarah as He had said, and the Lord did unto Sarah as He had spoken. For Sarah conceived, and bore Abraham a son in his old age, at the set time of which God had spoken to him. And Abraham called the name of his son that was born unto him, whom Sarah bore to him, Isaac.

—GENESIS 21:1–3

Faith, Truth, and Love

Faith is believing with your Heart, Mind, Body, and Soul
that Jesus Christ is our Savior and the first Son of God!
And that with love, God sent His first Son down
to His earth from His heavens high up above to
die for our wrongs and not rights with love.
Faith is believing that you're saved after being
washed clean by the blood of Christ.
Yes, you truly believe that your soul has been cleaned.
Faith is also believing it with plenty of bold,
for strength is faith in whole!
Truth is believing that Jesus Christ died
to save our lives, yes, our souls.
Believe me, He sincerely gave up His to give
us back ours, for truly life we had lost.
But God so loved we the world that He gave to
us His only begotten Son to pay the cost.
And believe me, it's truly, truly true that we're the
world He gave His only begotten Son to!
Love is God the Father, God the Son, and Love is also
God the Holy Ghost, who are One, yes, One Love!"
Love's also the most powerfulest force we have on earth for
Love is God who's nothing but Love, Love, and more Love.
Love is picking one up if they happen to be down; but no,
it's not pushing one father and farther to the ground.
With Faith and Truth, Love is caring, and caring is
something we all should do for all, true, but why?
For Right Is Faith, Truth and Love, Promising Love, That's Given
to Us All to Give to All from the Heavens High Up Above.
With Faith, Truth, and Love, Love, Yes, Let
Us All Love All and All You-al!

By *Jehovah* THROUGH THE HEART, MIND,
AND LEFT HAND OF ***Kevin Moss***

Wherefore laying aside all malice, and all guile, and hypocrisies, envies, and all evil speakings. As newborn babes, desire the sincere of milk of the world, that you may grow thereby: If so be you have tasted that the Lord is Gracious.

—1 PETER 2:1–3

I Wish, I Wish, I Wish!

I wish, I wish, I wish I'm wishing on a well, yes, I'm
wishing that I'm soon removed from this place of hell.
I ask if all these things I'm going through do I truly deserve; I
mean, in this life I'm living, have I made so many curves?
If I did, I'm sorry, Lord, for making these mistakes, but for
making them, should my life be lost just like tossed in a lake?
I wish, I wish, I wish I'm wishing on a star, wishing that
my day of release from this evil world isn't very far.
For on the day I'm released from the planet earth I'm
now living on, to me sometimes feels like hell.
I tell you that right then on that very day, my heart,
mind, body, and soul will ring like a bell!
For on that day, I'll truly be relieved of all the tears
that fall from my eyes every time I cry.
And then I'll be singing, just singing with so much joy, for then
I'll be rising to the heavens high, oh boy, oh boy, oh boy.
Now how about if I make my next wish
on a penny tossed up in the sky?
For remember high up above is where you'll find me at the
throne of God in heaven with my Lord, Jesus Christ.
I just pray that you all keep your eyes, ears, heart,
and mind wide, wide open at all times.
For believe me, all the wishes, yes, all the prayers we make
do go up to God, the Host of the heavens high.
And since by Him, all prayers are answered, don't
you think that's a good enough reason why?
To me, it is for Jesus Christ, who is our true Lord,
King, and Savior, yes, who was God in the flesh
also is He just the Greatest and the best.
And I don't know about you, but me, myself,
and I would never settle for anyone less!

By** Jehovah* THROUGH THE HEART, MIND, AND LEFT HAND OF ***Kevin Moss

Then said Jesus unto His disciples, if any man will come after Me, let him deny himself, and take up his cross, and follow Me.

—MATTHEW 16:24

We Too Are One

We must all face the fact that it's God's earth first, and it's
also a fact that God made this earth for all mankind.
Yes, for every one of us. And that means it's for
us both, the best of us and also the worse.
Yes, God made this earth for everyone of us, yes, for both me and
you. Yet it seems there's so many today that think they're so much
better than another, but instead of blessed,
they've been cursed forever, ever and ever.
But they're still our sisters or brothers, and that's because no
matter what's our race, creed, or color, we do all come together!
I mean, do we all not have a head that sits on our shoulder, and
does not red blood run through your body just like mine?
Yes, it does for it keeps our hearts pumping while
air blows through our bodies the whole time.
Which says again we really do come together, yes, truly we'll
always be sisters and brothers forever, ever and ever.
And I'm sure you know the reason for that is because we're all
human beings that's playing in the same movie, "LIFE."
The only difference is that we're all playing
in different scenes, alright?
Yes, you have your part, and I have mine but God's the Producer of
the whole show, and Jesus Christ is His eternal Director, you know?
It seems the problem is though that so many of we Actors and
Actresses are not playing the main part right, that's called LOVE.
And straight from the heart, we should have all been playing
the part of LOVE righteously from the very start.
Yes, just like God the Father, God the Son, and God the Holy
Ghost, who's again the Producer and Director of LOVE.
Yes, LOVE is the name of the whole show that
all started from high up above, you know,
So Everyone Remember Like God the Father, God the
Son, and God the Holy Ghost, We Too Are One.

By Jehovah THROUGH THE HEART, MIND, AND LEFT HAND OF ***Kevin Moss***

And now, Israel, what does the Lord your God require of you, but to fear the Lord your God, to walk in all His ways, and to love Him, and to serve the Lord your God with all your heart and with all your soul, To keep the commandments of the Lord, and His statutes, which I command you this day for your good? Behold, the heaven and the heaven of the heavens is the Lord's your God, the earth also, with all that therein is.

—DEUTERONOMY 10:12–14

Hide-and-Seek!

Hide-'N-Seek is a game that I remember most
children just loving to play when I was a child.
And it was such a fun game where we'd all
hide from another that had to seek.
Everyone who hid would continually peek, trying
not to be caught by the one that had to seek, but
surely someone would always get caught!
Yes, surely every time we played, someone lost by
being caught by the one who had to seek.
But it's funny today we find so many adults thinking like children
and with God they think they're playing hide-and-seek.
The problem is, God doesn't play games!
And if you try to play one with Him before you even
begin, you've already lost and have no win!
For God, our Heavenly Father, truly sees our every sin!
I keep telling everyone this because for our wrongs,
we'll all answer to God again, again, and again.
Because when it comes to God, He who
created both you and me who sin.
He also created all other human beings
that sin again, again, and again.
Yes, I keep telling all, so believe me, for
if you don't have Jesus Christ,
the Lord of Lords and King of Kings,
You don't have eternal life!
Now you may convince one of your friends to believe
you or maybe even a jury or fake judge,
but you'll never fool God from high up above.
Please remember what He said!
Yes, that what was said by He to all of we was "Thy Shall
Not Judge, for No One Can Judge Righteously but Me."
And believe me, He can, for He's the Breath of
Life, so He's in us all from the very start,

And since He's in us all, He sees every thought in our
minds and also feels every feeling in our Heart.
He hears every word out our mouths and has
seen our every action from our very start.
You see, this life we live truly isn't a game, and
God our Creator surely isn't a toy.
So believe me, everyone best start acting
like adults and not little boys.
I mean, I too, just like you wish, I could turn back
the clock to the very first beat, but we can't, so
we best stop acting like children playing

HIDE-AND-SEEK!

By Jehovah THROUGH THE HEART, MIND
AND LEFT-HAND OF ***Kevin Moss***

For mine eyes are upon all their ways: they are not hid from my face, neither is their iniquity hid from my eyes.

Jeremiah 16:17

For to be carnally minded is death; but to be spiritually minded is life and peace. Because the carnal mind is enmity against God: for it is not subject to the law of God, neither indeed can it be. So then they that are in the flesh cannot please God. But you are not in the flesh but in the spirit, if so be that the Spirit of God dwell in you. And if Christ be in you, the body is dead because of sin; but the spirit is life because of Righteousness. But if the Spirit of Him Who raised up Christ from the dead shall quicken by His Spirit who dwells in you.

—ROMANS 8:6–11

There is one law giver, who is able to save and destroy: who art thou that judgest another?

JAMES 4:12

Looks like I Have Nothing but I Have It All

The world laughs at me, at times saying I have nothing at all.
And when it comes to a lot of things of
this world, I guess that's true.
But I know I have Jesus Christ, and if you don't,
I also know I have more than you.
Now *Jehovah*, yes, *God*, who's our *Heavenly Father*,
owns all life, which means it all belongs to *He*.
But *He* gave it all to *Jesus Christ, His first Son*, and
that includes me, and I hope you too.
You see, when I was baptized into the body of Christ, I
became a true *son of Gods* through, and through.
So in my times of trouble or need by prayer in
the name of *Jesus Christ, Jehovah* do I call.
Now at times it may look like I have nothing,
but believe me, I have it all!
Remember, Jehovah is the creator of life, yes,
it's His, for it was all created by He,
Which includes the Heaven above, the Earth beneath, and the
Water under the Earth, which is part of the Great Blue Sea.
And let us not forget, It was also He that created
the sun, the moon, and every star you see.
Yes, it was *He* that made the fowl that fly in the air
and also the mammal that swim in the sea.
It was also our *Heavenly Father* that made
every animal, flower, bush, and tree.
And let us never forget that it was He that created both you and me.
And then after all His creating, He put we, man, above it all.
Now I know there's been times in your life that
you feel like you have nothing at all.
But believe me, if you just have Jesus Christ, you do have it all!

By *Jehovah* THROUGH THE HEART, MIND,
AND LEFT HAND OF ***Kevin Moss***

Now faith, is the substance of things hoped for, the evidence of things not seen. For by it the Elders obtained a good report. Through faith we understand that the worlds were framed by the word of God, so that things which are seen were not made of things which do appear.

—HEBREWS 11:1–3

Filled and Covered

To survive in this life we live today, we must at all times be
filled and covered with God, yes, Love, Love, and more Love.
Satan will attack you with his evilness at any time or any place
using anything, anyone, which means he'll use any face.
To defeat that beast and his followers, yes, those
of his taste and in spirit, his race, you must be
filled and covered with God, again Love.
Yes, you must be filled and covered with Love, for God, our
heavenly Father, is Love, and He loves us all at a regular pace.
So also must we just as He have a true
understanding of love and grace.
You see, Satan is after every soul he can get,
which are the souls of yours and mine.
Yes, he is, so that we also play a part in helping him
to fill that big black hole, do not you see?
And if we do, we're never washed clean by the
blood of Christ, the Lord of Lords and King of
Kings, nor are we set free by He eternally.
Believe me, as it's better to be safe than sorry, it's also better
to be filled and covered with Love and not of Worry!
So at all times be filled and covered, yes, yes, yes, oh yes,
yes, yes, always be filled and covered with Love.
Yes, Be Filled and Covered, Filled and Covered, Just Filled
and Covered with God, who's Love, Love, and More Love!

***By** Jehovah* THROUGH THE HEART, MIND
AND LEFT-HAND OF ***Kevin Moss***

The wolf also shall dwell with the lamb, and the leopard shall lie down with the kid; and the calf and the young lion and the fatling together; and a little child shall lead them. And the cow and the bear shall feed; their young ones shall lie down together: and the lion shall eat straw like an ox. And the sucking child shall play on the hole of the asp, and the weaned child shall put his hand on the cockatrice' den. They shall not hurt nor destroy in all My holy mountain: for the earth shall be full of the Knowledge of the Lord, as the waters cover the sea.

—ISAIAH 11:6–9

Now You're Truly One

We pray here today that no one ever comes
between what God has brought together.
No, no one, for now they're truly one!
Now I ask you both to listen and believe. In this marriage, you're
going to have both your ups and downs and your ins and outs.
Yes, you shall have both good and bad days
for that's just another part of life.
This you're to remember and hold in your heart.
FOR NOW, YOU'RE TRULY ONE!
Now you both have paid the price, yes, for you've paid
the wage of marriage and you've paid with your lives.
Which Makes Him Yours and You His.
AND NOW, YOU'RE TRULY ONE!
I now first say to her, "He's the head," and then
I say to him, "And she's your right arm!"
FOR AGAIN, NOW YOU'RE TRULY ONE!
And then most importantly, I say to you
both, please let God be the referee!
No matter what took you down or brought you
up or what pushed you out and pulled you in, or
whether your day has been good or bad.
Believe me, as long as you sit down at the table together as a
team, which you now are, through Love a team that is also one.
And as one team while sitting at the table together as one, if you
let God be the referee, believe me, He'll give you the solution!
YES, HE WILL, FOR THROUGH HIM,
LOVE, NOW YOU'RE TRULY ONE!

***By** Jehovah* THROUGH THE HEART, MIND,
AND LEFT HAND OF ***Kevin Moss***

The wife has not power of her own body, but the husband: and likewise also the husband has not power of his own body, but the wife.

—1 CORINTHIANS 7:4

Time's Running Out

Time is running out, and it's going by awful fast; yes, we're
coming to the end for the beginning doesn't last.
Believe me, to the end of time we shall shortly be, so
let us all repent to God; yes, let us make our plea.
Believe me, time is really running out, and truly that's no joke.
Sometimes I just can't believe that just yesterday I was only
in my twenties, and already here today I'm in my fifties.
To me, it really seems unreal that I'm already a fifty-year-
old man and believe in my life before time runs out,
I best come up with a new and better plan!
Well, the best plan unto me has truly come to be giving my
life back to God for He has set me free to live eternally.
Yes, believe me, time, time, time is really running out, and this
do I say to all, so yawl believe me without a single doubt.
You know today it seems we have more earthquakes, tornadoes,
and all kinds of floods just about every single day.
Now tell me with all your heart, do you truly
believe it's supposed to be this way?
And just about how many more things today must happen
like this, before we all are gone without a single miss?
Now I believe God, our Heavenly Father, is giving us warning
signs of the arrival of His first Son every day, would not you say?
Yes, and I think it's about time for us to get our lives in
order right on down to the grind, yes, I must say.
And please remember what I've said, yes, just keep it in your heart
and on your mind that we truly, truly, truly are running out of time.
YES, WE TRULY ARE FOR TIME'S RUNNING OUT!

***By** Jehovah* THROUGH THE HEART, MIND,
AND LEFT HAND OF ***Kevin Moss***

And that knowing the time, and now is high time to awake out of sleep: for now is our Salvation nearer then we believed. The night is far spent, the day is at hand: let us therefor cast off the works of darkness, and let us put on the armor of light.

—ROMANS 13:11–12

You Are What You Eat

Unfortunately, yes, we are what we eat!
What our Lord once said is so very true; yes, it was very true
what He said when He said to both me and you, which was,
"It's Not What Goes in the Body That Defiles
It, but It's What Comes Out!"
But still you are what you eat, and that's no doubt.
Now let's see if I can explain this to you in an easier
way, but still letting you know what it's all about.
When Jesus Christ said it's not what goes in the
body that defiles it but what comes out,
I believe He meant things like Cursing, Threatening,
Fighting, and Killing and just plain Evil Thoughts,
For these are the kind of things that defile the body; He also
meant the inner body and not the out, yes, your soul!
But when I say You Are What You Eat, I'm speaking on
things like eating pork or eating too much sugar
Or things like using drugs, drinking alcohol, or smoking cigarettes.
Yes, for when you eat and use these kinds of
things, it's things like it you become.
And on top of that, you're defiling the outer body, yes, your flesh.
So may we all learn to eat the Word of God for
we're then eating the body of Christ.
And please believe me for that's a treat that's oh so nice.
YES, IT IS, SO PLEASE ALWAYS REMEMBER,
YOU ARE WHAT YOU EAT!

***By** Jehovah* THROUGH THE HEART, MIND,
AND LEFT HAND OF ***Kevin Moss***

But He answered and said! It is written man
shall not live by bread alone, but by every word
that proceedeth out of the mouth of God.
—MATTHEW 4:4

Testimony, Praise, and More Praise

I testify my love to God, but through His first
Son, He first testified His Love to me.
Now Jesus Christ's testimony was as clear as day,
and it was thick and surely not thin.
For His testimony was when He died on a cross
for us all, for nothing else but love, you-al.
And This may we remember inside our heart, for
it truly wasn't a loss but surely was a win.
And for all the love He showed us then, with Love
may we all show our love back to Him?
Yes, by learning to love all again, again, and again. And
let us start by giving it to our Heavenly Father.
To Jesus Christ, our Lord and Savior, Who's His First Son, and to
the comforting Holy Ghost with praise, praise, and more praise.
Now we could never praise Him too much; in fact for
all He's done, we couldn't praise Him enough.
No, all we can do is just praise Him, praise Him, and praise Him,
yes, every single one of us, just praise Him more and more.
Remember, all praise is His, and it will always be His
forevermore, and this we best believe, and truly that's for sure!
Now I want to give you my testimony, which
is true through, through, and through,
which is that I belong to Jesus Christ; yes,
truly, truly, truly I do, I do, I do.
And that's from my head to my toe, my left to my right,
my front and my back, and my ins and my outs.
Yes, all of me belongs to Jesus Christ without a singe doubt.
And all these things I say from my heart, mind,
body, and soul in the name of Jesus Christ.
Also in His name do I truly, truly thank Him again, again, and
again, and here I end my testimony with "Amen, Amen, Amen."

By** Jehovah* THROUGH THE HEART, MIND, AND LEFT HAND OF ***Kevin Moss

For if I do this thing willingly, I have a reward: but if against my will, a dispensation of the Gospel is committed unto me. What is my reward then? Verily that, when I Preach the Gospel, I may make the Gospel of Christ without charge, that I abuse not my power in the Gospel.
—1 CORINTHIANS 9:17–18

There's Two Sides to Every Story

Heads or tales, just what side of the coin has
really turned out to be yours?
And just who have you really come to be in
this life we live today, night or day?
Remember, there's two sides to every story.
That's right two sides to every story and to every story two sides,
Which means the right team to be on could be His or his.
You see, one day we'll all come live in the
Heavens High or the hell below.
And then you'll be walking on pure, pure gold
living eternally in Happiness, Peace, and Joy.
Or you'll be locked away in hell in a blazing fire
eternally with nothing but blue, and that's so true.
Now your cup could seem empty but end up
being full until it's running over.
Or it just may seem like you've got it all and
your cup is oh so full wall to wall.
But then you glance back at that cup again that you thought
was so full, and you see now that it's nothing but empty.
And on top of that, the only thing running down
it is your sweat and misery drip by drip.
Now I say this to all the world for it's so very true; yes, it is,
believe me, this could happen to me and also to you!
Also, true it is that there's two sides to every story and the
story on one side of the coin is Happiness, Peace, and Joy.
Or you may get the other side, which is nothing but
blue, blue, and more blue, but that's up to you.
So tell me just which side of the coin has
really turned out to be *yours*?
AS WELL AS *YOURS, YOURS,* AND *YOURS!*

***By** Jehovah* THROUGH THE HEART, MIND,
AND LEFT HAND OF ***Kevin Moss***

The Rich Man and Lazarus

There was a certain rich man, who was clothed in purple and fine linen, and fared sumptuously every day: And there was a certain beggar named Lazarus, which was laid at the gate, full of sores. And desiring to be fed with the crumbs which fell from the rich man's table: moreover the dogs came and licked his sores. And it came to pass, that the beggar died, and was carried by the Angels into Abraham's bosom: the rich man also died, and was buried; And in hell he lift up his eyes, being in torments, and seeth Abraham afar off, and Lazarus in his bosom. And he cried and said, father Abraham, have mercy on me, and send Lazarus, that he may dip his finger in water, and cool my tongue; for I am tormented in this flame.

—LUKE 16:19–24

True Is the Heart

As true as love does dwell in the heart.
It's also true that God has loved us all, yes,
His Creation, from the very start!
Yes, God so loved we the world oh so much that He gave the
life of His only begotten Son just to save the lives of ours.
TRUE IS THE HEART
Here we find flying star after star.
Yes, we do for here Jesus, Christ the Lord of Lords and
King of Kings, willingly gave His life just to save ours.
And just for that reason alone, shouldn't we all learn
to love all, all, and all like flying sparks?
Yes, we should for love has always been so
true in it's self from the start.
TRUE IS THE HEART!
Now we find Love, Love, and more Love
in the light and in the dark.
Yes, we really, really do, so let all hearts leave upon
another's heart that same exact mark, yes. Love.
FOR TRUE IS THE HEART!

***By** Jehovah* THROUGH THE HEART, MIND,
AND LEFT HAND OF ***Kevin Moss***

And shall come forth; they who have done good, unto the Resurrection of Life; And they who have done evil, unto the Resurrection of Damnation.

—JOHN 5:29

TRUE IS THE HEART!

Nothing Else but Love!

You know, our Heavenly Father really doesn't want that
much from us; no, He really doesn't, not at all.
But yes, He does want us to be more like He spot by
spot, everywhere we go to, everyone we see.
And the spot He wants us to be and leave on everyone
everywhere we go is no One else but He.
Yes, Love, Love, and more Love, you see?
NOTHING ELSE BUT LOVE!
Love is something we all want and need for God is Love and it's
our best plea to show everyone Love, to prove our Love to He.
Yes, we're all to Love all with nothing else but Love, do not you see?
Our Heavenly Father has so many times picked us up in
our most times of need whenever we called on He,
The Bright Shining Light to plant a seed.
Now we're to do as He and help others up if they happen to fall,
yes, so true with Love we are, yes, with Love we are to be indeed.
NOTHING ELSE BUT LOVE!
Remember, it was God that made three different elements
in six days and named them Heaven, Earth, and Sea.
And with nothing else but Love, He made these
three elements just for YOU and ME.
He then created everything of life in these elements
and then gave life to what He had just created.
Yes, He did, from the stars in the sky down to the green grass
below, you know, you know, yes, you know that it was so, SO?
So we should all see this clearly for it's as clear as day
that He did it all with nothing else but Love.
Once again just for YOU and ME, Okay!
Yes, Okay, so we're all truly also to be just like
He, full, full, full just full of Love.

YES, FULL OF NOTHING ELSE BUT LOVE, TRUE?

By** Jehovah* THROUGH THE HEART, MIND, AND LEFT HAND OF ***Kevin Moss

THESE ARE THE THINGS THAT YOU SHALL DO.

Speak you every man the truth to his neighbour; execute the judgement of truth and peace in your gates: And let none of you imagine evil in your hearts against your neigbour; and love no false oath: for all these are things that I hate, says the LORD.

—ZECHARIAH 8:16–17

The Truth, the Truth, the Truth Is Nothing but the Truth!

The truth, the truth, the truth is nothing but the truth!
The truth will be, yes, always be the one that truly sets us free, right?
Yes, that's right, for the truth is our Lord, Jesus Christ,
our Savior and our King, the Bright Shining Light.
Now sometimes the truth does really hurt, but a lot of times, it
takes hurt to make us clearly see we're nothing else but dirt.
But we can call on God through Jesus Christ, and God can and
will remove the dirt from our heart with just a single burp.
That's the truth, and the truth is the truth as
a liar is a liar and a thief is a thief
Who both thrive, thrive, and thrive to break another's peace.
Believe me, for this they do, they do, yes, they do, now tell
me, tell me, please tell me, don't you think that's true?
Sure it is for the only one that constantly changes
their story over, over, and over is a liar, true?
But Why?
For you can't change the truth and the truth doesn't change,
so a liar just tells lie after lie over, over, and over.
And believe me, a thief will steal from anyone, even their
own Dad or Mother, as well as their Sisters and Brothers
just as they would another. Now all of this is
nothing but the truth, the truth, the truth.
Now I ask you all to tell me, tell me, yes, tell me, isn't that the truth?

***By** Jehovah* THROUGH THE HEART, MIND,
AND LEFT HAND OF ***Kevin Moss***

Now Listen!

And if any man think that he knows anything, he knows nothing yet as he ought to know. But if any man love God, the same is known of him.

—1 CORINTHANS 8:2–3

True?

Do You Think You Can?

He, yes, He did create the Heavens, the Earth, and the Great
Blue Sea; yes, it was all created by He, just for you and me.
It was, yes, it was in just six short days, yes, it and so much
more was created by He again just for you and me.
Believe me, it and so much more He did create, as the stars in the
sky that are so high that so many you see and some you don't see.
And after creating them, He put each star where He wanted it to be.
He also created and placed in the sky both the
sun and the moon along with every cloud.
And on top of that, HE created the snow and rain
that seem to fall from those clouds somehow.
Now do you think you understand, or must I say it all again,
but if you think you've got it, I now ask you this, my friends!
Of all the things He does now, on top of what He did back
then, I Ask you all the world to tell me, please tell me,
DO YOU THINK YOU CAN?
In those same six days, He also created every kind of fowl!
Yes, those that fly with wings high in the sky
and those that walk the ground.
Now here we have two different kind of birds, yes, fowl, again
those that fly with wings and those that walk with feet.
And some we can't, but most of them are just so delicious to eat.
Plus, in those same six days, He also created every
other kind of animal and every kind of beast.
Oh yes, of their quality it was He that
created the best and also the least.
Yes, it was *Jehovah* that made every kind of
flower, bush, as well as every kind of tree.
Plus, every kind of fruit and vegetable that grows from thee.
Now Satan, that evil Devil, yes, he that brought
evil into the world will never defeat God.
Believe me, he won't tomorrow just like he can't today
for the same exact reason he couldn't yesterday.

So once again, I ask you all the world to
tell me, tell me, please tell me,
REALLY, DO YOU THINK YOU CAN?

By *Jehovah* THROUGH THE HEART, MIND,
AND LEFT HAND OF ***Kevin Moss***

For who in the heaven can be compared unto the Lord? Who among the sons of the mighty can be likened unto the Lord? God is greatly to be feared in the assembly of the Saints, and to be had in reverence of all them who are about Him. O Lord God of Hosts, who is a strong Lord like unto You? You have broken Rahab in pieces, as one that is dead; You have scattered Your enemies with Your strong Arm. The heavens are Yours, the Earth also is Yours: as for the world and the fulness thereof, You have founded them.

—PSALM 89:6–11

You, even You, are to be feared: and who may stand in Your sight when once You are angry?

—PSALM 76:7

Our World Tomorrow

The first and only Father, yes, God, the Father of Love, is truly also the Father of Life.

Now we, Dads and Mothers of today, must, as our Heavenly Father, teach and show the children of today, who'll be our world tomorrow, Love. Yes, we must teach them how to Love with Love, Love, and more Love just like we must teach them right from wrong while singing the same song, Love. For (1) time just goes by so fast; yes, it does, for so quickly yesterday has become today and just as quick today will be tomorrow. And that means if we really love our children today, then with love, through love, and for love, we'll get them in order ("NOW!"). And that's because for (2) they're our world tomorrow, which means as we're their parents today, tomorrow they'll be parents too, Okay? And if God allows it at that time, we'll be happy grandparents, for the table does turn just as they say. Alright, my friends, we now come to fact number 3, which is it's truly our job to teach them right from wrong today, would not you say? That's right today, just as it will be their job to teach our futures, future right from wrong tomorrow. And last but surely not least, always remember and never forget their our world tomorrow who's truly the best, oh yes, yes, yes. And also don't forget their world tomorrow will be our world tomorrow, tomorrow, and tomorrow, so for them all, let's do our best!

By** Jehovah* THROUGH THE HEART, MIND, AND LEFT HAND OF ***Kevin Moss

All unrighteousness is sin: and there is a sin not unto death. We know that whosoever is born of God sinneth not; but he that is begotten of God keepeth himself, and that wicked one toucheth him not.

—1 JOHN 5:17–18

SO JUST LOVE THEM ALL WITH LOVE, LOVE, AND MORE LOVE!

Gone but Not Forgotten

There's so many today that for the moment has
left us, yes, they're now resting in peace.
But for the same moment, not one of them has been forgotten!
And that's because God forgets none but holds all in His heart.
Yes, on the inside of the heart of God are we all protected, by His Love.
Believe me, everyone that's been washed clean by
the blood of Christ has also won eternal life.
But we've also gained from He, the right to be a member in
the heart of God with His loving protection eternally.
So it may seem to you that the Lord Jesus Christ,
yes, God is gone and, to some, forgotten.
But believe me, believe me, please believe me, He'll soon be
coming back through the clouds to reclaim what is His! And
this may we always hold in our heart with Faith, Hope, and
Joy remembering that one may be gone, gone, yes, gone.
But Even Though That One Is Gone!
We Still Must Always Hold in Our Heart, and Remember
in Our Mind, That in the Heart of God Not One Is
Forgotten. Yes, Some Are Gone, but Not One Is Forgotten!

***By** Jehovah* THROUGH THE HEART, MIND,
AND LEFT HAND OF ***Kevin Moss***

For the Lord knoweth the way of the righteous: but the way of the ungodly shall perish.
—PSALM 1:6

Wake up, Everyone, for You Most Be Sleeping

Wake up now, world, for you must be sleeping; yes, you must be, if you don't see every day more and more that we the world are truly sinking. Wake up, wake up, wake up, world, for you should know He's at the door, just from all the different signs going on all around us; I know this for sure. I also know we better wake up for we're truly running out of time!
And when we do, just like them of Noah's time, we may also lose our minds, for truly just as they were, it seems we too are
ALSO SLEEPING.
So wake up, do I tell everyone in the world, yes,
wake up and stop so much sleeping!
Open up your eyes, for they must be closed if you don't see all the changes being made today, and it's all happening do I say.
YES, IT IS RIGHT UNDER OUR NOSE'S, OKAY?
So many of these changes you should see, like it being in the twenties in July and the sixties in February, aren't you kind of worried? Worrying you should be doing, yes, worrying that you're on the right team, for we're truly in the last days.
I'M SURE YOU KNOW WHAT I MEAN!
The day just seems like it's getting shorter and shorter, and it must be, because now time goes by oh so fast, scene by scene, it just doesn't last. So I tell all the world once again that you best wake up, you best wake up for believe me,
WE'RE TRULY COMING TO THE END.
I know at the start in the beginning of the show, it felt oh so good just like you were in a dream, you know?
But believe me, oh world, for I tell you the truth, we're now in the last scenes, yes, for time has just about run out,
YOU KNOW WHAT I MEAN?
As He said it is so true, yes, that in this world, the last days shall be dark for both me and you and you too!

And it seems like today most of our dreams are nightmares, so wake up, world, I say once again for we truly are coming to the end, *So Please Wake Up, Everyone, and Stop Sleeping, all My Friends.*

By** Jehovah* THROUGH THE HEART, MIND, AND LEFT HAND OF ***Kevin Moss

> And that, knowing the time, that now it is high time to awake out of sleep: for now is our salvation nearer than when we believed. The night is far spent, the day is at hand: let us therefore cast off The works of darkness, and let us put on the armour of light.
>
> —ROMANS 13:11–12

We Have Another Chance

We all make mistakes, and sometimes we seem to
fall, but by the Blood and Love of Jesus Christ,
Another chance has been given to us all!
You know, like the first time you tried to walk, someone
was there at your rescue to catch you if you'd fall.
In the same exact way, Jesus Christ, the Saving Messiah,
will be there at our every call if we ever happen to fall.
May we all remember that death is just another part of
life and is something that we all shall experience.
And not by just a glance.
But through Jesus Christ, the first Son of God who's
our Savior, we've been given another chance.
So if at first you don't succeed try, try again with Jesus Christ at
the wheel who's your everlasting friend and will always be a win.
Believe me, to have a friend like Jesus Christ is a blessing and a gift.
Yes, it is, for one, He's the One that will always be
there to help you if you ever happen to miss.
So don't let life's problems put you in a bind or trance!
But always remember in the heart that through
Jesus Christ, you have another chance.
For God the Father so Loved we the world that He
gave us the life of His only begotten Son.
And He the Son so loved His Father, and plus we His world
who He so truly loved that He paid with His blood!
For just as the Father He too has the same kind of Love.
So let Him take your life out of the trance it may be in.
And believe in your heart that through Jesus Christ,
you have another chance with a sure-enough win.

***By** Jehovah* THROUGH THE HEART, MIND,
AND LEFT HAND OF ***Kevin Moss***

The burden of the word of the Lord in the land of Ha'-drach, and Damascus shall be the rest thereof: when then eyes of man, as of the tribes of Israel, shall be toward the Lord.

—ZECHARIAH 9:1

Are You Ready?

I ask you all, are you ready, Yes, ready?
Please tell me, tell me, yes, tell me, are you ready?
That's ready for the second arrival of our Lord, Jesus Christ!
Also, are you ready for the day your number shall
be called, yes, the day you lose your first life?
Now I know a thousand years is nothing but a few
moments to God, yes, just another day.
But I also know that we're not God, no, we're not;
we're just images of His likeness, am not I right?
Which means all of us that's not ready, better
get ready since we're not God.
Every day that goes by means we're running out of time.
And That's Why!
DO YOU UNDERSTAND WHAT I'M SAYING?
I MEAN, DON'T YOU SEE THE LIGHT?
WHY?
DON'T YOU SEE THE SIGNS?
Then dig this—
"THE ONLY WAY TO THE FATHER IS
THROUGH HE JESUS CHRIST, THE SON!"
Alright?
AND I END BY ASKING EVERYBODY ONCE
MORE, JUST WHAT I ASKED YOU BEFORE.
SO TELL ME, ARE YOU READY?
YES, TELL ME, ARE YOU READY OR NOT?

***By** Jehovah* THROUGH THE HEART, MIND,
AND LEFT HAND OF ***Kevin Moss***

Therefore the fathers shall eat the sons in the midst of thee, and the sons shall eat their fathers; and I will execute judgments in thee, and the whole remnant of thee will scatter into the winds.

—EZEKIEL 5:10

Walking the Golden Sidewalk

Walking the Golden Sidewalk, I pray one day to do.
For walking the Golden Sidewalk will take away all my blue.
Didn't God once tell everyone, meaning all His girls
and boys, that walking the Golden Sidewalk
would bring you nothing but happiness, peace, and joy? Yes, He
told us all the world that whoever walks the Golden Sidewalk would
walk it with Happiness, Peace, and Joy. But first you'll have to get
back to heaven and, through the Golden Gate, my boy. And for
that you'll need Jesus Christ, who Loves we all the world, and don't
forget but remember that it's truly His world. Now Jesus will always
be our way through life, as well as our lift up to heaven and also
our key through the Golden Gate. For He's the only way up, and
since He's the key, He's also the only way in again, again, and again.
Yes, He is, for only through the blood of Christ are
we truly set free, now, just as we were back thin.
And remember and don't forget once again both
the heavens and the earth belong to He!
Now in heaven where the sidewalks are gold, also are the homes
made of diamonds, rubies, and pearls, I tell all the world.
I pray one day that we all make it up to heaven to walk
the Golden Sidewalks of Happiness, Peace, and Joy.
Now I end by asking all to take a moment and think about
what a day that's going to be; yes, it'll be just a joy.

AND WITH LOVE AND PEACE DO I SAY OUT
LOUD TO ALL, OH BOY, OH BOY, OH BOY!

***By** Jehovah* THROUGH THE HEART, MIND,
AND LEFT HAND OF ***Kevin Moss***

And who is he that will harm you, if ye be followers of that which is good? But and if you suffer for righteousness' sake, happy are ye:

AND BE NOT AFRIAD OF THEIR TERROR, NEITHER BE TROUBLED;—worried.

—1 PETER 3:13–14

Wrong, Wrong, Wrong, Is Nothing Else but Wrong

Wrong is just wrong, and it's nothing else but wrong!
And right will always be right just like it'll always be bright, alright?
So we must learn to follow God's commands, for Satan will
tell you right is wrong and wrong is right whenever he can.
And believe me, you-al, that will be again, again, again, and
again; yes, he'll be just telling you to sin, sin, sin, and sin.
AND SINCE SIN IS WRONG, WRONG, WRONG,
IT'S SURE NOT A WIN, MY FRIENDS.
But you can win, yes, through Jesus Christ, my friends, you
can win, win, win, yes, just win again, again, and again.
For Jesus Christ, who to us, the Father did send is a good Friend
and a good Son, for in our times of need He did come.
And let's not forget that also through His
blood for us all He surely won.
SO WRONG IS JUST WRONG, WRONG, WRONG,
AND NOTHING ELSE BUT WRONG, ALRIGHT?
But Jesus Christ saved our lives through His own blood, right?
So don't do wrong, do right, for wrong is just wrong,
wrong, wrong and nothing else but wrong!
NOW ISN'T THAT RIGHT, OR IS IT ALSO
WRONG, WRONG, WRONG?
YES, IT'S RIGHT, RIGHT, RIGHT, AND
NOT WRONG, ALRIGHT!

***By** Jehovah* THROUGH THE HEART, MIND,
AND LEFT HAND OF ***Kevin Moss***

When I was a child, I spake as a child, I understood as a child, I thought as a child: but when I became a man, I put away childish things. For now we see through a glass darkly; but then face to face: now I know in part; but then shall I know even as I'm known.

And now abideth faith, hope and charity, these three; but the greatest of theses three is charity.

—1 CORINTHIANS 13:11–13

Over and Over Again

Over, over, and over, again, again, and again
do we go through ups and downs.
Which means at times in life it's not so easy, but
hard, and I'm not fooling around.
Yes, sometimes life can be so hard, I mean hard sometimes life really
can be, and sometimes it's just about as hard as a rock if you ask me.
Do you know what I mean, yes, you know how you feel on
one of those days you just feel like you're going to pop?
Well, before you do that, my friends, please remember.
Yes, remember for it's just the truth, with a sure-enough win.
And that's that God loves us all over, over
and over again, again and again!
Now that should lift you up with joy, my friend,
and my friends, friends, and friends.
So just keep looking up to all those days to
come with happiness, peace, and joy.
Again, again, and again, my boy, my boy, my boy.
But if one of those down, down days should happen to slip back
into your life again, remember, remember, and remember.
Yes, Remember That God Truly, Truly Loves You Over, Over, and
Over with Nothing but Pure, Pure Love Again, Again, and Again!

***By** Jehovah* THROUGH THE HEART, MIND,
AND LEFT HAND OF ***Kevin Moss***

The wages of sin is death; but the gift of
God is eternal life through Jesus Christ, our Lord.
—ROMANS 6:23

He That Sinnith Not Cast the First Stone

Truly, my people, Paul did once say in the book of ROMANS 3:20–23,
We all fall short of the glory, and there's not
one good man left, no, not one.
Now if you think you're one that hasn't done any wrong,
then as Jesus Christ said, go 'head and cast the first stone.
But I tell you that you best be careful before you cast that stone!
And you better be sure you've done nothing
but right and not a single wrong.
For believe me, sin is in us all, and believe me once again,
this means that we do come together wall to wall.
And that's because when Adam, the first human being, did sin,
he, that first human being, also put sin and death into we all.
And that means one day we all shall fall when our number is called.
There's only been one perfect and good man
that has ever walked this earth!
And remember what He said, "Don't Call Me Good, for No
One's Good but My Father," for He never did wrong.
SO HE THAT SINNITH NOT GO AHEAD
AND CAST THE FIRT STONE!

***By** Jehovah* THROUGH THE HEART, MIND,
AND LEFT HAND OF ***Kevin Moss***

If we say that we have no sin, we deceive our selves, and the truth is not in us.

—1 JOHN 1:8

If we say that we have not sinned, we make him a liar, and his word is not in us.

—1 JOHN 1:10

Where Are We Now?

For our love and also my loneliness, which I feel so real in my heart.
My mind continues to drift back and forth from me to you.
It seems you're not there, but I'm still here and
feel so lonely and blue without you.
Sometimes I stop and ask myself, is this real love I feel or
just some kind of a dream that I wish to be loved?
And at times I must say that I really don't know, for one
minute, it seems like we're getting so much closer.
But then it seems like we're drifting farther and farther apart!
Yet through all the traveling our minds have gone together, it
seems we've still not found what we're looking for, or have we?
You tell me, for it seems I no Longer know!
Now once upon a time, I really thought I knew and loved you,
but now I sit in my dark room and lay my head in my lap.
And there you find me just wondering, wondering,
and wondering just who you really are.
I once thought I was the apple of your eye and the star of your mind.
But it looks like I'm just a speck of dust that was once in your heart!
But you've seemed to have opened its door and
have just let our love blow away, but why?
For that answer I'm just wondering, wondering, and wondering,
Yes, I'm Now Just Wondering, Where Are We Now?

***By** Jehovah* THROUGH THE HEART, MIND,
AND LEFT HAND OF ***Kevin Moss***

Whose adorning let it not be that outward adorning of plaiting the hair, and weaning of gold, or of putting on of apparel; But let it be the hidden man of the heart, in that which is not corruptible, even the ornament of a meek and quiet spirit, which is in the sight of God of great price. For after this manner in the old time the holy women also, who trusted in God, adorned themselves, being in subjection unto their own husbands:—submissive.

—1 PETER 3:3–5

Who Said We Can't or Won't When We Already Are?

Who said we can't get along when just with love we can on, on, and on?
Who said we won't make it to heaven together when, just with
Love, Love, and more Love, we'll all be singing a new song?
And who said we can't and won't be Brothers
and Sisters when we already are?
For We All Come Together No Matter Your Race,
Creed, or Color, No Matter Who You Are!
Who said we can't do right but must do
nothing but wrong, wrong, wrong?
Just who said we won't ever learn to love one another
and get along like Sisters and Brothers?
Believe me, we can, and one day we will!
For We All Come Together No Matter What Race,
Creed, or Color, No Matter Who You Are.
Yes, we can, and one day we will for Brothers and Sisters
we really, really are, and that's the way we're to feel.
FOR REAL!

***By** Jehovah* THROUGH THE HEART, MIND,
AND LEFT HAND OF ***Kevin Moss***

> Finally, be ye all of one mind, having compassion one of another, love as a brethren, be pitiful, be courteous: Not rendering evil for evil, or railing for railing: but contrariwise blessing; knowing that ye are thereunto called, that ye should inherit a blessing.
>
> —1 PETER 3:8–9

May I Kiss His Every Toe

I so much look forward to that special, special day, everyone.
And I do believe with all my heart that day is soon to come.
Yes, that special, special day that I may kiss every toe upon His feet.
For God's feet and His every toe Is truly
another part of Him, you know?
Yes, His every toe is a toe upon one of God's feet; yes, it is His
every toe, but the problem is, His name is Jehovah though!
Now Jehovah is the Greatest, just the Greatest and the
only God there is, ever was, and ever will be!
And Jehovah, yes, God does brightly glow!
And so does His feet and every one of His toes.
So may I kiss His every toe, then slide over to the right, and
cry my tears of joy over the feet of our Lord, Jesus Christ.
For, yes, He sits on the right side of Jehovah, yes, God, His Father,
and believe me, everyone, Jesus Christ is truly His First Son.
So let every tear of joy that falls from my eyes also
fall upon His feet so like Mary Magdalene!
I, too, may also wash His feet with my hair, you know what I mean?

***By** Jehovah* THROUGH THE HEART, MIND,
AND LEFT HAND OF ***Kevin Moss***

And He turned to the woman, and said unto Simon, Seest thou this woman? I entered into thine house, thou gavest me no water for my feet: but she has washed my feet with tears, and wiped them with the hairs of her head.

—LUKE 7:44

The Comforter

There's another name that was given to the
Holy Ghost a long, long time ago.
I'm sure some of you as myself will be surprised that
of His other name, how many just don't know.
Now while we're speaking on His other name,
may I also give you another fact?
Which is that the other name that was given to
Him, believe me, He really does do just that!
Now those that do not know it, both him and her, I
now give it to you all, my sisters and brothers.
Yes, He really does have another name, which
is COMFORTER, all my friends.
It's just so amazing that the first day that He the Comforter
enters into your temple, yes, your human flesh,
You automatically acknowledge that He the
Comforter is both the greatest and the best.
Now I tell you from the bottom of my heart that
everything I'm telling you is truly, truly the truth.
For instance, when you receive the COMFORTER,
He, our Heavenly Father, has just reentered you.
Believe me, you'll feel such a difference when He
first steps into your heart, BUT WHY?
Because He shall, at that very moment, heal your every sore,
solve your every problem, and fulfill your every want.
So now do you see why He was also given
another name called Comforter?
Now there's nothing else in life but He that
can make you feel like His, Love.
Believe me, I truly do love the name Holy Ghost, but I get so much
comfort from Him that I love calling Him Comforter the most.

***By** Jehovah* THROUGH THE HEART, MIND,
AND LEFT HAND OF ***Kevin Moss***

Who is going into heaven, and is on the right hand of God; angels and authorities and powers being made subject unto Him.

—1 PETER 3:22

Christ, Head of the Temple and King of God's Army

The body of Christ is the first and main temple.
Now God our Creator said that those who are washed clean by
the blood of Christ, and has accepted Jesus Christ as their Savior,
Have also come to be a body part of He the first Temple.
For Christ does save by washing one clean of all sin with His
Blood and then you really do become one of His body parts.
And once you've become a member of the
body of Christ, you're truly His!
As the different parts of our bodies play a role
in helping our bodies to function
Now since we're a member of the body of Christ, we're to play a role
in helping His body to function by spreading His Love and Word.
Yes, as the different parts of our bodies have a job to do, we now,
being a member of the body of Christ, also have a job to do.
Now God, our heavenly Father, makes nothing
for nothing and nothing with nothing,
Which means we're all given a gift of some kind from He.
Now let's say he was given the gift of preaching the Word
of God and she the gift of teaching God's Word.
And another was given the gift of helping the elderly
and the young and the sick or the poor.
No matter what the gift or job that God has
given you is, it still must be done.
First of all, Jesus Christ, God in the flesh is the first and
main temple, and we're to be bricks of that temple.
Yes, we're bricks of God's first temple, and
we're also soldiers in God's army.
YES, WE'RE NOW ANOTHER SOLDIER IN HIS ARMY!

***By** Jehovah* THROUGH THE HEART, MIND,
AND LEFT HAND OF ***Kevin Moss***

For as we have many members in one body, and all members have not one same office: So we, being many, are one body in Christ, and every one members one of another.

—ROMANS 12:4–5

Let Jesus Get You Over, Across, and Through

You know some loads in life that we sometimes
have to carry can really be heavy,
And on top of that, some goals we set for ourselves
to accomplish in life can be pretty hard.
So what's the best way to accomplish these kind
of goals in life or carry these kind of loads?
I'd Say to Let Jesus Get You over, across, and through.
Do you know what I mean? That's right, just let Jesus
get you over the hump and all the bumps.
For even if it feels as hard as climbing over a
wall, believe me, He'll get you over.
Even if Life feels as heavy as carrying a ton
over a hole, He'll still get you over,
Or maybe it feels as hard as trying to get around a stumbling block.
Through prayer and faith, Jesus can and will get
you over, across, through, and around.
Yes, and He'll catch your every fall before you even hit the ground.
So whatever your case may be, just let Jesus get you over,
across, and through by truly setting you free right now.
Please believe me, for these are things that only He
can do, and truly, my friends, this will always be.
For Jesus Christ Is both the lift and the key for you, me, and all of we!

***By** Jehovah* THROUGH THE HEART, MIND,
AND LEFT HAND OF ***Kevin Moss***

Watch. And Pray, That Ye Enter Not Into Temptation: The Spirit Indeed Is Willing, But The Flesh Is Truly Weak.

—MATTHEW 26:41

Eight-Ball Corner Pocket

You know at times life can be a real drag, and
sometimes that causes us to miss a lot of points.
I know I missed a lot of them by not always being
too smart and letting a lot them just fly by.
Yes, there's been so many that I've missed
that I could make a long, long list.
Now with a lot of us, the important ones
that would have surely been a hit.
It seems we didn't understand or just didn't get.
But believe me, if you just have in Him faith the size
of a mustard seed, you can move a mountain.
Now since I'm about ready to end the game, I call eight-
ball corner pocket, which is nothing but a gain.
But for some people, it may take some time and a few falls.
Yes, to see that to win in the game of "LIFE" and
to always have one to catch you if you may fall,
you only have one that you can always call.
So to me, what you do first, for it's the best thing
to do is yes, join the winning team.
Plus, don't take so many chances, but be smart and
pull up your pants, if you know what I mean!
Now I hope you know and believe that in the
game of life, there's only one winning team.
Again, again, and again. I hope you
understand and know what I mean!
Yes, join the winning team, and let Jesus Christ,
the Lord of Lords and King of Kings, with His
and our heavenly Father, "God," with the
twinkle of an eye, turn your whole life around, for with His
Love does He change your life's every scene, scene by scene.
This I know, for when I joined the winning team,
it seemed I started making every shot I took.

For instance, look at the way that eight ball is
flying down the table. LOOK, LOOK!
I mean, I started winning so many games that at times I felt like a crook, but through Jesus Christ, I know I'm a winner. So just as before, here I go again; yes, I call eight-ball corner pocket on all you sinners and beginners.

By** Jehovah* THROUGH THE HEART, MIND, AND LEFT HAND OF ***Kevin Moss

Wherein they think it strange that ye run not with them to the same excess of riot, speaking evil of you: Who shall give account to Him that is ready to judge the quick and the dead.
—1 PETER 4:4–5

A MEMBER OF THE WINNING TEAM!

These Perilous, Perilous Days

For some reason in these days, it just seems to be oh so
dangerous out here in this world for us all, you know?
And what bothers me the most about that is, it seems like
you're in danger both when you come and when you go!
Yes, it seems just about every day you find someone that's
fallen in harm's way, yes, another one every single day.
And what hurts the most about that is that it seems innocent
little children get hurt the most, would not you say?
Well, God did say in the second book of Timothy
that they'll be Perilous Days Where People Will
Love Only Themselves and Money.
And today it's so scary and sad; plus, it hurts oh so bad how so
many people lose out by burning, burning fires, I must say.
Then we have another one here that really doesn't
care, for when one was down, they didn't try to
help that person up as one that cares.
No, they didn't try to help that person up with love like they cared,
for they were another one of those perilous people who don't care.
But God did say it would be this way in the Perilous Last
Days when people would love only themselves and money.
Yes, it's just crazy in the world today, yes,
just crazy in any and every way.
I mean just for money, a plain piece of paper, so
many are robbed and killed every single day!
With guns and in so many cars, trucks, trains, and plains, so many
times another's life is taken in these last and Perilous, Perilous days.

***By** Jehovah* THROUGH THE HEART, MIND,
AND LEFT HAND OF ***Kevin Moss***

This know also, that in the last days perilous times shall come. For men shall be lovers of their own selves, covetous, boasters, proud, blasphemers, disobedient to parents, unthankful, unholy, Without natural affection, trucebreakers, false accusers, incontinent, fierce, despisers of those that are good, Traitors, heady, highminded, lovers of pleasures more than lovers of God; Having a form of godliness, but denying the power thereof: from such turn away.

—2 TIMOTHY 3:1–5

It's God's Word That Stands

There's so many people today that believe they're still standing
tall, but in the eyes of God, they've truly made a fall.
Yes, they really have, so instead of rising up to heaven in spirit,
Down to hell all of them shall fall!
And believe me, truly they will fall, yes, into a big black hole
because they wouldn't listen and follow all of God's laws.
Now we have those that don't like, believe, or
agree with God's laws, yes, I know.
But since He's God, our Creator, when it comes to life, He created all!
For He's God, so truly is He Life, and if you don't follow
His commands and laws, believe me, you truly will fall.
But just by doing His Will and following His laws,
He'll pick you up and dust you off with nothing
but Love, and this He'll do for us all.
So always let it be God's law that stands out in your heart,
mind, body, and soul by being there at His every call.
And always remember with love that it was God that
gave you life and this did He do for us all.
But even though God gave you life, without our Lord,
Jesus Christ, His First Son, you still shall fall.
This do I say to all again, again, and again for He's the only
way up to heaven, and believe me, He's also the only way in.
So be washed clean by the blood of Christ and enter the
Golden Gates of Heaven and have yourself a ball.
But always remember what was once said by
Jesus Christ, God's first Son, which was,
"Man doesn't live by bread alone but by every word
that proceeds out of the mouth of God."
For bread feeds the flesh and God's Word feeds the soul!
And feeding your soul with God's Word will do
nothing but make you whole, whole, and whole.
So always let it be God's Word that stands out
in your Heart, Mind, Body, and Soul.

By** Jehovah* THROUGH THE HEART, MIND, AND LEFT HAND OF ***Kevin Moss

See that ye refuse not him that speaketh. For if they escaped, not who refused him that spake on earth, much more shall not we escape, if we turn away from Him that speaketh from heaven.
—HEBREWS 12:25

The Door of Doors

You know today we have so many doors we use to come in and go out of.
Also in the world today I believe we have way too many paths,
streets, roads, and highways we use to travel on, would not you say?
Sure, you would, but didn't Jesus Christ say that we were to pick up
our cross and follow He up the narrow path going the right way?
But far too many times we find ourselves going another
way; that's surely not the right way, which is His way.
And with that, what the main problem half the time comes
to be is that we don't even know where we're going.
Now can anyone truly tell me right now the true and exact
time and age we're living in or when God first made man?
No, I don't think so, for how do you know what the time and age is
now or when it all will end if you don't even know when it all began?
Now I believe all the crazy and mixed-up things we
see happening these days all around us are just signs
of the last days; remember what He said!
YES, JESUS DID SAY, "WHEN YOU SEE THESE
SIGNS, KNOW I'M AT THE DOOR!"
Believe me, God is so good and has so much
Love that He's giving us warning signs.
Yes, warning signs that our Lord Jesus Christ is truly on His way.
And heaven's door has already been opened
and closed, you know what I mean?
That means He's already come through one door.
YES, FOR HEAVEN'S DOOR IS THE FIRT DOOR OF DOORS.
And when He comes through the next door, THE Door of Clouds,
the trumpet will be blown, so I ask all the world, are you ready?
I then tell you all, oh wide, wide world, you best be sure it's so
important that I tell you again once more that you best be sure!
Yes, you better be, for if you're not, I feel sorry
for ye, for it won't be long before our Lord Jesus
Christ Will be back to reclaim what is His.

Now I ask you again once more to believe me, for He'll soon be coming through; yes, back through He'll soon be coming.
"YES, COMING THROUGH THE DOOR OF DOORS!"

By** Jehovah* THROUGH THE HEART, MIND, AND LEFT HAND OF ***Kevin Moss

> For we have not followed cunningly devised fables, when we made known unto you the power and coming of our Lord Jesus Christ, but were eyewitnesses of His majesty. For He received from God the Father honor and glory, when there came such a voice to Him from the excellent glory,
>
> This is my beloved Son, in whom I am well pleased.
>
> And this voice which came from heaven we heard, when we were with Him in the holy mount. We have also a more sure word of prophecy; whereunto ye do well that ye take heed, as unto a light that shineth in a dark place, until the day dawn, and the day star arise in your hearts:
>
> —2 PETER 1:16–19

A Little Water on My Tongue

Fire heats it up, but water cools it down, and as
water cools it down, fire still burns it up.
Up, up, up does the fire surely blow, and down to
hell in that fire shall all sinners go, you know?
Oh Father Abraham, Please Have Mercy on Me.
Send Lazarus Down That He May Dip His Finger
in Some Water and Cool My Tongue.
FOR I'M TORMENTED IN THIS FLAME!
The fire shall be high, and it shall be hot; it won't be going
out, and whoever falls in it won't be getting out.
BUT AS MY FATHER SAID, YOU SHALL ETERNALLY BURN!
Oh Father Abraham, Please Send Lazarus Down That He
May Dip His Finger in Some Water and Cool My Tongue.
FOR I TELL YOU, IT'S HOT DOWN HERE!
AND I JUST NEED A LITTLE WATER ON MY TONGUE!

***By** Jehovah* THROUGH THE HEART, MIND,
AND LEFT HAND OF ***Kevin Moss***

For in many things we offend all. If any man offend not in word, the same is a perfect man, and able also to bridle the whole body.

Behold we put bits in the horse's mouths that they may obey us; and we turn about their whole body.

—JAMES 3:2–3

Even so the tongue is a little member, and boasteth great things.

Behold, how great a matter a little fire kindleth!

—JAMES 3:5

In Six Days

In only six days did God make the Heavens,
the Earth, and the Great Blue Sea.
And with Love, Love, and more Love, He also
made everything else of life that you see.
All this was just a little bit of work for God,
and for God, it was pretty easy too.
But tell me, don't you believe it would have been a lot
more harder, if not impossible, for me or you to do?
That's right, it would have been so much harder,
harder, and harder for either one of us to do!
Yes, it would have been just as hard for us to do then as
it is for man now to stop, stop, yes, stop doing sins.
But for God, who made it all in just six days, it was easy!
So He rested after He had inspected what He had just created.
And everything that God made was "GOOD"; believe me, it
all was oh so good, truly it was, yes, truly wave after wave.
And let us never forget that once again He did it all in just six days.
Now if you try and tell me of another that's as good as
that, I'll call you a liar, and believe me, that's a fact.
BUT WHY?
For you can't show me another who can create three elements and
plus everything of life in these elements in six days, can you?
NO, YOU CAN'T, AND ONCE AGAIN, DON'T
FORGET, HE DID IT ALL IN SIX DAYS.
YES, IN JUST SIX DAYS, HE DID IT ALL,
FOR ME AND YOU, TRUE?
YES, IT'S TRUE, TRUE, TRUE!

***By** Jehovah* THROUGH THE HEART, MIND,
AND LEFT HAND OF ***Kevin Moss***

And the word of the Lord came unto me saying, Son of man, set thy face toward the mountains of Israel, and prophesy against them, And say, Ye mountains of Israel, hear the word of the Lord God; Thus saith the Lord God to the mountains, and to the hills, to the rivers, and to the valleys; Behold, I, even I, will bring a sword upon you, and I will destroy your high places. And your alters shall he desolate, and your images shall be broken: and I will cast down your slain men before your idols. And I will lay the dead carcases of the children of Israel before their idols; and I will scatter your bones round about your altars.

—EZEKIEL 6:2–4

Another Beautiful Day

It's through God that we have some very beautiful, beautiful days.
And really some of them are really just that
beautiful, would not you say?
Yes, they're just as beautiful as the bright shining
sun in every way; what a day, what a day.
Jehovah, yes, God the Father makes such beautiful days
that it makes me say, as Fat Albert would always say,
HEY, HEY, HEY!
Yes, it's so beautiful today for once again He
shines His Love down on all of we.
Yes, He does on another one of His beautiful days in every way.
On top of that, so many beautiful things are grown by the
power of His, yes, through His bright powerful sun every day.
Like all the beautiful flowers and trees that grow with ease as He
blows His Love through the air like a nice cool breeze everywhere.
YES, IT'S REALLY BEEN Just ANOTHER
BEAUTIFUL DAY, I MUST SAY!

***By** Jehovah* THROUGH THE HEART, MIND,
AND LEFT HAND OF ***Kevin Moss***

And the Lord God took the man, and put him into the garden of Eden to dress it and to keep it.

—GENESIS 2:15

A Mother's Love

A MOTHER'S LOVE IS SO SPECIAL,
SWEET, TENDER, AND SOFT.
AND IN MOST OF OUR TIMES OF TROUBLE AND
NEED, HER LOVE USUALLY PAYS THE COST.
I REMEMBER THOSE TIMES MOM WOULD CRADLE ME
THEN SOFTLY ROCK ME TO SLEEP.
AND WHENEVER SHE'D HEAR MY CRY, SHE'D
PICK ME UP IN HER SOFT, STRONG ARMS.
FOR HER LOVE JUST WENT THAT DEEP,
SO NOW DO I SEND UP TO HER, YES, TO YOU, MOM,
I SEND THESE WORDS OF THANKS
FOR ALL YOUR LOVING CARE.
AND THAT'S BECAUSE ALL MY LIFE,
WHILE YOU WHERE HERE,
NO MATTER WHAT I DID, YOUR LOVE
WOULD STILL BE THERE.
I GUESS IN MY EYES, MOM WASN'T AN APPLE
BUT A PEACEFUL, LOVING SPARK.
AND SHE WAS SO SPECIAL TO ME THAT
THIS I KNOW, YES, I KNOW!
I KNOW MY LOVE WASN'T NEVER ENOUGH
FOR HER SOFT, SWEET, LOVING HEART,
SO TO YOU, MOM, DO I SAY THESE WORDS,
HOPING TO DRAW BACK THAT SPARK.
TO YOU, MOM, WITH ALL MY HEART
AND FROM THE BOTTOM OF IT.
BELIEVE ME, I'LL ALWAYS LOVE YOU, AND
YOU'LL ALWAYS HAVE MY HEART.

***By** Jehovah* THROUGH THE HEART, MIND,
AND LEFT HAND OF ***Kevin Moss***

Honor Thy Father And Mother, That Thy Days May Be Long Upon The Land Which The Lord Thy God Giveth Thee.

—EXODUS 20:12

How Can One Not Love, Love?

Love is the most beautiful and powerfulest force we have on earth,
And Love will make the best starting from the worst.
Believe me, there's really nothing that love can't overcome.
And that's because Love is God the Father, God
the Son, and God the Holy Ghost.
3 that equals 1!
Yes, Love has been sent down to us from high up above.
SO SOMEONE TELL ME, HOW CAN ONE NOT LOVE, LOVE?
Please someone tell me, tell me for I just don't understand.
So would you please tell me, how can one not Love, Love my man?
For it's Love that soothes the heart, it's also love that lifts you up.
Yes, lifts you up on those days that you feel so down and oh so dark.
It's Love you feel in your heart when you're
with that one who draws the sparks.
Yes, that one you hold in your arms oh so tight
who lit that fire inside your heart.
You know, the one that turned your heart
from cold ice into flying sparks.
And just for that reason alone do I ask this question to all the world,
Which means every man, woman, boy, and girl.
How can one not Love, Love the true one that's
always there for you when you call?
Remember You-al Love, Love, and more Love
Was, Is, and Will Always Be.
So with Love I Ask You all Once Again, How
Can One Not Love, Love, You Tell Me?

***By** Jehovah* THROUGH THE HEART, MIND,
AND LEFT HAND OF ***Kevin Moss***

And the fruit of righteousness is sown in peace of them that make peace.

—1 PETER 3:18

NOW THAT'S REAL LOVE!

Who Gave the Most

Has the thought ever passed your mind of just who gave the most?
So many say they gave a lot but didn't.
No, they just told lie after lie with a whole lot of boast.
Now there's so many that claim they gave so much.
But just what have you gave? Yes, just what was your DOSE?
Some gave money, and some gave anger with a whole lot of hate.
But if you just give love, that'll be oh so great!
Think about it though, and ask yourself, then just tell me.
When it comes to giving love, why are you always so late?
I remember reading a scripture in the book of Mark 12:41
That, in disguise, was just love, you know?
People do cast money into the treasury:
And many that are rich, to them cast in much.
But this poor woman cast in just two cents.
And to so many, what she cast in was the less.
But to God, our heavenly Father, yes, the
Host believed she cast in the most
And also cast in the best
Because with love, she cast in her very, very last.
Yes, that was all she had, but she still cast it in happy and not sad
For what she cast in, she cast in with love, love, and more love,
And when you've given with Love, believe me, you've given your all.
So God, the Heavenly Father, Yes, He Himself Says with
Love, and Remember, Everybody, Again He's Our Host.
And Believe Me, He Said Whoever Gives Out
Real Love Has Truly Given the Most!

***By** Jehovah* THROUGH THE HEART, MIND,
AND LEFT HAND OF ***Kevin Moss***

And He saw also a certain poor widow casting in thither two mites. And he said, Of a truth I say unto you, that this poor widow hath cast in more than they all: For all these have of their abundance cast in unto the offerings of God: but she of her penury hath cast in all the living that she had. – poverty.

—LUKE 21:2–4

Thank You, Thank You, Thank You

THANK YOU, THANK YOU, THANK YOU,
SHOULD WE all DO AND SAY!
Now Let us all first thank God for giving us the Lives we Live, Okay?
And we should also thank Him for the bodies
we live in, again, again, and again.
SO THANK YOU, THANK YOU, THANK YOU, MY
HEAVENLY FATHER AND MY BEST, BEST FRIEND.
We should then thank Jesus Christ, God's first
Son, who gave His life to give us back one.
Yes, He died on the cross for us all; I mean He truly paid the cost.
Yes, He paid the wage of sin for us all; yes, He
did, so He the Son truly is the Boss.
So let us all thank Him, thank Him, yes, thank
Him over and over again and then some.
Now we must also thank all the Doctors,
the Mechanics of the human flesh,
And also all the Nurses with all the others
working in Hospitals, oh, yes, yes, yes.
Yes, the Hospitals that keep our bodies
functioning for truly they're the best.
SO TRULY DO I THANK YOU, THANK YOU,
THANK YOU all, OH YES, YES, YES!
Let's also thank the Firemen that get oh so wet while putting out
fire after fire, and for just that do I thank them; yes, that's a bet.
And let's thank all the Policemen who are the Long Rangers of today.
Yes, let's thank them for keeping us safe from
all the criminals in our world, okay?
Also, thank all the Bus Drivers, Pilots, Conductors, yes,
all the Captains of all the different kinds of ships.
These are the different people that get us
around the world every single day.
And always remember and never forget the
first thanks goes up to God, Okay?

Yes, thank God, for He made the earth we walk on and then made we the World who's been God's worse.
NOW WE SHOULD ALWAYS GIVE THANKS TO EVERYONE, BUT PLEASE JUST REMEMBER TO ALWAYS THANK GOD FIRST.

By** Jehovah* THROUGH THE HEART, MIND, AND LEFT HAND OF ***Kevin Moss

But seek ye first the kingdom of God, and his righteousness; and these things shall be added unto you.

—MATTHEW 6:33

Ho, Ho, Ho

"Ho, ho, ho" Is what Santa does say.
Yes, when he flies through the air in his sled
of gifts for us all on Christmas Day.
And he delivers his beautiful gifts with nothing but
Love, Love, and more Love on such a special day.
Yes, the day of Christmas, a day of love, which
really is so nice, would not you say?
Remember, this day is the day of birth of our Lord, Jesus Christ.
Believe me, it was just for love that Jesus Christ,
the first Son of God, was born just to die.
(Now Wasn't That Nice?)
Yes, it was just oh so nice because He did it
all for love, yes, love that's right.
And plus to show us how to get to heaven, yes,
just for love He really paid the price.
So let us all ho, ho, ho with love for another Christmas Day,
Truly another birthday of our Lord, Jesus Christ, the One
that, for us all with love, gave up His Own Life.
And after He gave up His, He also gave we the
World what He had just lost, yes, LIFE.
So once again, let us all ho, ho, ho with love on
Christmas, the birthday of Jesus Christ.
So Ho, Ho, Ho; Ho, Ho, Ho; Ho, Ho, Ho; and Ho, Ho, Ho.
YES, JUST LET EVERYONE HO, HO, HO TO ANOTHER
MERRY, MERRY CHRISTMAS, YOU KNOW?

By *Jehovah* THROUGH THE HEART, MIND,
AND LEFT HAND OF ***Kevin Moss***

And therefore it was IMPUTED TO HIM FOR RIGHTEOUSNESS. Now it was not written for his sake alone, that it was imputed to him; But for us also, to whom it shall be imputed, if we believe in him that raised up Jesus our Lord from the dead'. Who was delivered for our offenses, and was raised again for our justification.

—ROMANS 4:22–25

"The Whole Armor of God" Ephesians 6:14–18

(1) The Belt of Truth

The belt of truth holds you up from beginning to end. And as it holds you, it also carries you from end to beginning all over again. Yes, truth is oh so strong that it gives you chance after chance, what also holds you up, yes, it does hold you up just about as wall as your belt holds up your pants.

(2) The Breastplate of Righteousness

This must we wear at all times. Yes, we must wear the breastplate of righteousness for the battle we're fighting isn't against man, no, but the battle is against that evil beast, who, with love, I just can't stand.

(3) The Sandals of the Gospel of Peace

We should always be wearing these sandals, for we all wish to be at peace, don't we? Yes, we do, starting from the highest down to we the least!

(4) The Shield of Faith

With faith, this shield will protect you from that evil beast's temptations as well as his fiery darts. Please believe me, world, and I hope I'll draw a spark. Yes, a spark by telling you that beast Satan is so evil that as he'll aim for your head, he'll also aim for your heart. So again believe me, as I asked you before! For by having the shield of faith, you can take the smile from Satan and put it on your own face.

(5) The Helmet of Salvation

May we all wear this helmet, for truly do we all need salvation. But why? Because salvation is deliverance! So let us put on the helmet of salvation and be delivered by Christ. For if we first do all we can in saving and delivering ourselves, oh yeah, Yeah, yeah. God will deliver us with a glorious salvation from all the Temptations, Trials, and Corruptions of this evil world.

(6) The Sword Is the Word of God
Pick up your sword, yes, the Word of God, and Study, Learn, and Memorize it. Live by these words, and once again, you will be protected. For all of God's words are so sharp that they'll cut that beast and all his followers straight down the heart.

"AND LAST BUT SURELY NOT LEAST WE HAVE!"

(7) The Supernatural Provision Prayer
May We All Put on the Prayer Cloth by Constantly Saying,
"OUR FATHER IN HEAVEN, HALLOWED BE YOUR NAME. YOUR KINGDOM COME, YOUR WILL BE DONE ON EARTH AS IT IS IN HEAVEN. GIVE US THIS DAY OUR DAILY BREAD. AND FORGIVE US OUR SINS, FOR WE ALSO FORGIVE EVERYONE WHO IS INDEBTED TO US. AND DO NOT LEAD US INTO TEMPTATION, BUT DELIVER US FROM THE EVIL ONE. Amen, Amen, Amen!"

By** Jehovah* THROUGH THE HEART, MIND, AND LEFT HAND OF ***Kevin Moss

Cast Him under Your Feet

We all should be on that journey up that narrow path!
And believe me, while we are at times, it may get hard.
And it may get as hard in some of our futures
as it's been in some of our pasts
But remember when he tries you, you're to follow the
steps of Jesus Christ and cast him under your feet.
Yes, our Lord Jesus Christ surely won, for He did defeat that evil beast.
In full, yes, in full, He did overcome and surely won.
And everyone who has accepted Him by deciding to follow
Him, then like Him, eternal life you too have won.
Remember, it went as so when the tempter tempted Jesus Christ, he said.
If you be the Son of God, turn this rock into
bread, and Jesus Christ said,
"Man does not live by bread alone, but by every word that
proceeds out of the mouth of God" (MATTHEW 4:4).
The devil then took Him to the top of a temple and said,
"If you be the Son of God, jump down to the ground
and God's Angels will catch you when you fall."
"But Jesus Christ told him "No" for you don't
tempt God at all" (MATTHEW 4:7).
Then that dirty beast took Him to the top of a
mountain saying "Just bow down, bow down, and
worship me and I'll give you all you see."
But Jesus said, "Get thy hence, Satan for thou shalt worship the
Lord Thy God and only He shalt thou serve" (MATTHEW 4:10).
And He then cast him under His feet, but
didn't that beast have a lot of nerve?
May everyone hold this in their heart and mind, remembering
like Jesus Christ to always keep that same beat.
And whenever that evil one tries you, you're to do just as
our Lord Jesus Christ and cast him under your feet!

By Jehovah THROUGH THE HEART, MIND, AND LEFT HAND OF ***Kevin Moss***

Because the law worketh wrath: for where no law is, there is no transgression. Therefore it is of faith, that it might be sure to all the seed; not to that only which is of the law, but to that also which is of the faith of Abraham; who is the father of us all.

—ROMANS 4:15–16

No Matter How Many Times You Fall

You know there's so many things in life today that seem to make
us fall, and so many times we do that it may fill like wall to wall.
And just as it was back then, it still is today!
But there's still one you can call in those hard times if you happen to fall.
Yes, there is One you can call that goes by the name of Jesus
Christ that will pick you up and dust you off at your every call.
And That's No Matter How Many Times You Fall!
Now there's so many times in our life we feel like nothing but failure,
But thanks be to God we have the Saving Messiah.
Yes, given to us was Jesus Christ, the Savior, truly the
Saving Messiah, who's the first Son of God.
It's His Love that's real and strong, and it's also His Love that will
love us with pure Love, Love, and more Love on, on, and on.
So remember, you-al, with faith, whenever
you may fall, it's He that you call.
And with Love, He'll help you up all, all, and all.
AND ONCE AGAIN, THAT'S NO MATTER
HOW MANY TIMES YOU FALL!

***By** Jehovah* THROUGH THE HEART, MIND,
AND LEFT HAND OF ***Kevin Moss***

When Jesus saw him lie, and knew that he had been now a long time in that case, he saith unto him, Wilt thou be made whole? The impotent man answered him, Sir, I have no man, when the water is troubled, to put me into the pool: but while I am coming another steppeth down before me. Jesus saith unto him, Rise, take up thy bed, and walk. And immediately the man was made whole, and on the same day was the sabbath.

—JOHN 5:6–9

Your Eyes Are Open, But You Still Not See

It seems today we have so many that are blind, yet they see.
Believe me, if you're spirally blind, you see not
the light of God, meaning you're truly, truly blind
and can't see the light at all, but why?
No, you won't see Eternal Life in the day or the night for
you first didn't see God when He shined His Light.
Now in the flesh, which is the physical you, do
you see all the beautiful flowers in the grass as
you see the clouds in the sky up so high?
But still you're blind; now let me tell you why!
Because just like you have a physical body, you also have a spiritual
one too, and believe me when I say, truly that's the real you!
And you only can see the Light of God through
Your spiritual eyes; believe me, for it's true.
YOUR EYES ARE OPEN, BUT YOU STILL NOT SEE!
You see, you must be able to see the Light of
God or you're nothing else but blind.
Yes, blind living in darkness and just keep walking into walls,
doors, and tables and things of that likeness just lost in time.
There's only One that can open our spiritual eyes, and that's
God, the Holy Ghost, through our Lord Jesus Christ, alright?
And that's because God the Father, God the Son, and God the
Holy Ghost are truly, truly One, yes, One Shining Light.
In the book of GENESIS 1:26, God the Father said to Jesus Christ,
His first Son, "Let Us Make Man in Our Image and Likeness."
And again believe me, God's Image and Likeness is Spirit, not
Flesh, so the way you see God is with your spiritual eyes, alright?
And that means if your physical eyes are open but your spiritual
eyes are closed, you're still blind, and that's what I mean when I say,
"YOUR EYES ARE OPEN, BUT YOU STILL NOT SEE!"
AND Jesus Did Say, "If the Blind Lead the Blind,
They Both Shall Fall in the Ditch!"

By** Jehovah* THROUGH THE HEART, MIND, AND LEFT HAND OF ***Kevin Moss

And when they agreed not among themselves, they departed, after that Paul had spoken one word, Well spake the Holy Ghost by E-sa'-ias the prophet unto our fathers, Saying GO UNTO THIS PEOPLE, AND SAY, HEARING YE SHALL HEAR, AND SHALL NOT UNDERSTAND; AND SEEING YE SHALL SEE, AND NOT PERCEIVE: FOR THE HEART OF THIS PEOPLE IS WAXED GROSS, AND THEIR EARS ARE DULL OF HEARING, AND THEIR EYES HAVE THEY CLOSED; LEST THEY SHOULD SEE WITH THEIR EYES, AND HEAR WITH THEIR EARS, AND UNDERSTAND WITH THEIR HEART, AND SHOULD BE CONVERTED, AND I SHOULD HEAL THEM.

—ACTS 28:25–27

Three Different Flavors with One Delicious Topping

A cream has been offered to us all, a cream
that will fill your life with love.
And will whip, whip, whip your life until the
love in your life is just oh so thick.
Now this cream comes in three different flavors, and God gives you
every single flavor with such a delicious topping truly nice and thick.
Yes, you can have His ice cream flavors: Happiness, Peace, and Joy.
With His delicious toping, called Love, if
you'll just let Him into your life,
He'll then blend your Heart, Mind, Body and
Soul by fully turning your life around.
And then with Love, He'll truly make your life
oh so safe and truly, truly sound.
Believe me, God can and will truly make your life safe and sound.
Yes, when through His Blood and Love, Like a
blender, He turns your life around.
I say these words through God and for God,
to every Male and Female do I say.
Yes, to every girl and boy, so believe me, my
sisters and brothers with joy, joy, joy.
In time your life will be oh so sweet that anyone who
comes near you would truly think that you were Dairy
Queen, and your love they'll just eat, eat, eat.
God's Power and Loving Grace makes you feel
happy and puts smiles on your face.
Yes, it gives nothing but Happiness, Peace, and
Joy with Love by God's Loving Grace.
So Don't Ever Forget About God's Topping for It's Surely a Plus.
Yes, a Plus That He Calls Love, Love, and More
Love That He Just Gives to All Of Us.

By** Jehovah* THROUGH THE HEART, MIND, AND LEFT HAND OF ***Kevin Moss

Cast out the scorner, and contention shall go out; yea, strife and reproach shall cease.
—PROVERBS 22:10

ISN'T IT JUST DELICIOUS?

He's So, So Real, and It's Oh So True

Truly, truly, truly it is just so true.
Yes, it is, and also true is it that this applies
to we all, yes, to both me and you!
Please believe me, believe me, believe me for it really does apply to us all.
For since He's God, yes, life, isn't He in us all, all, and all?
God does give life to all of we; yes, He's in us all, True?
YES, HE IS BECAUSE HE'S SO, SO
REAL, AND IT'S OH SO TRUE!
Yes, true it is that heaven is God's home!
For heaven is where He placed His throne and made it His home.
Heaven's where you'll find nothing but Happiness, Peace, and Joy.
And it will be coated with Pure Love, and that's for sure.
For in heaven you find nothing but Pure Love
for God is Love, Life's true cure.
Yes, Love, Love, and more Love, and He's oh so pure.
It's also very true that Jesus Christ is the only Savior of Life.
Plus He's the first Son of God, who's also
both our Brother and Savior too.
AND BELIEVE ME, HE'S OH SO REAL,
AND THAT'S OH SO TRUE!

***By** Jehovah* THROUGH THE HEART, MIND,
AND LEFT HAND OF ***Kevin Moss***

He that oppressed the poor to increase his riches, and he that giveth to the rich, shall truly come to want.

—PROVERBS 22:16

We All Come Together, for Truly We Are One

Yes, we do come together for we're all human beings, yes, One.
But the main reason we come together is because, like God, we
too are spirit, so together we do come, you know what I mean?
For instance, isn't the true body of God spirit and
is also His true image scene by scene?
Even though once His scene did change from Spirit to Flesh and
then back to Spirit from Human Being, so Spirit is the main scene.
And that's because we started off spirit and in spirit, we shall
end for spirit we really are; again, do you know what I mean?
But just in case you don't check out this scene!
We find in the book of GENESIS 1:26 "And God said, let
us make man in our own image and in our own likeness."
And since God's image is spirit, ours is too, right? And
from you, I know that's a Yeah and not a No!
For years now, man has been fighting, because so
many believe one's race is better then another's.
But remember, our true image is the image
of God do I say one to another.
Yes, That Means Our Real Image Is Truly
Spirit, All My Sisters and Brothers!
Meaning our race is spirit too, which means both
me and you; now the spirit has no color as Black
and White for it's either dark or bright.
You see, the spirit is a shade, so if you're following God, your
spirit is bright like He, and if you're not, it's as dark as can be!
Yes, it's either dark or bright and not black or white, for dark or
bright are just not colors as black and white but arc shades, alright?
Now since we're all spirit like God, my sisters and brothers let us all
learn how to Love, Love, and more Love everyone, yes, each other.
For Remember, We All Do Come Together; Believe
Me, We Do, Which Means We Are One.
AND THAT MEANS, ME AND YOU, AND THEN SOME!

By Jehovah THROUGH THE HEART, MIND, AND LEFT HAND OF ***Kevin Moss***

And God said, Let Us make man in Our Image, after Our Likeness: And let them have dominion over the fish of the sea, and over the fowl of the air, and over the cattle, and over the earth, and every creeping thing upon the Earth, So God created man in His Own Image, in the image of God created He him; male and female created He them.

—GENESIS 1:26–27

How Can One Go a Day without God?

How can one go a day without God. I Just don't know, do you?
I know I can't for it was God who created the air I breathe, the
food I eat, and the plants that make the clothes upon my back.
Truly was it then and truly is it now, so let's get to that, that it was
God that created the Heavens, Earth, and Sea and not you or me.
Yes, three different elements did God create for all of we.
Believe me, it was God that created both the Sun and the Moon
and placed every Star that you see where He wanted it to be.
So How Can One Go a Day without God? I Just
Don't Know, but If You Do, Then You Tell Me!
Don't you know that God is in everything of life that we see?
Yes, He is, for God is life, which includes both you and me.
And yes, He's in every beautiful flower coming up from the ground;
And He's in every bush, flower, and tree, no fooling around.
He's also in every fowl with wings that fly
high up in the sky just everywhere.
God's also in every kind of mammal that swims in the sea; once
again, I tell you He's in everything of Life, including you and me!
So How Can One Go the Day without God? That I Just
Can't See, So How One Does It, Don't Ask Me!

***By** Jehovah* THROUGH THE HEART, MIND,
AND LEFT HAND OF ***Kevin Moss***

And God said, Let the waters under the heavens be gathered together unto one place, and let the dry land appear: and it was so. And God called the dry land Earth; and the gathering together of the waters called He Seas: and God saw that it was good.

—GENESIS 1:9–10

We're Truly, Truly Blessed

I do believe that it's so true that through the Love, Mercy, and
Grace of God, we've been truly, truly blessed, don't you?
Yes, it's so true for God has shown us nothing but
Love by taking away from us so much blue.
Yes, God of the heavens, who also made the earth, has so
much Love that as He's given to me, He'll also give to you.
So repent and give Him His Praise, and just like that, with the
twinkle of an eye, He'll take your life right out of its maze.
Yes, He can, and He will by turning your life
around and making it just as sweet as glaze.
And then you'll feel no more haze in your life; no, you won't feel
nothing except wanting to give God praise, praise, and more praise.
BELIEVE ME, YES, BELIEVE ME, WE'VE
BEEN TRULY, TRULY BLESSED THROUGH,
THROUGH, AND THROUGH.
He first blessed us with the Heavens, and
there He placed His throne.
He then blessed us with several other planets, the
Earth being one, and it He made our home.
And then He blessed us with the Sun, the
Moon, and every Star you see.
He followed it by blessing us with all kinds of beautiful
Flowers, Bushes, and some of the most loveliest Trees.
The mist is the air we breathe, and in the mist, we find flying so
many beautiful Birds and Bees; what a breeze, what a breeze.
We also have so many Rivers all connecting back to the Great Blue
Sea and so many lovely streams all made just for you and me.
We were also blessed with all kinds of Mammals that
swim in all those Rivers, Ponds, and Seas.
Yes, the Mammal is such a blessing for those we eat are oh
so delicious; plus, good for the brain are those we eat.

The Point Here Is Once Again by the Love, Blood, Mercy, and Grace of God Truly by He the Greatest and the Best We've All Truly Been Blessed. BELIEVE ME, WE HAVE, OH YES, OH YES, OH YES, BELIEVE ME, WE'VE TRULY, TRULY BEEN BLESSED, BLESSED, AND BLESSED!

By** Jehovah* THROUGH THE HEART, MIND, AND LEFT HAND OF ***Kevin Moss

And when they heard it, they glorified the Lord, and said unto him, Thou seest, brother, how many thousands of Jews there are which believe; and they are all zealous of the law.

—ACTS 21:20

Who Cast Down Who?

There's a question that I must ask today, but it seems to me
there's so many that don't know the answer, would not you say?
But there's just so many people in the world today, so I guess some may.
So I must ask this question; now someone tell me, tell me,
yes, tell me just who cast who down, would you say?
Now remember, God's the Heavenly Father and God's truly the
Son and God's also the Holy Ghost, Three that equal One!
Yes, God's the Creator of Life, and on His right side,
when He created the Heavens, Earth, and Sea, believe
me, His first Son, stood right next to He.
Yes, His true first Son, Jesus Christ, truly did stand right next to He.
And Satan, who's now the Devil, was at that time
an angel who went by the name of the Fourth
Star and was God's right-hand man.
But the problem was, instead of him praising God as he should
have been, unfortunately, my friends, he had another plan in mind.
Now his plan was first convincing God's angels to give
all their praise to he and not to God, you see?
He then told God's angels to bow down, bow
down, bow down, and worship me,
Telling them, "No, don't worship God, worship
me!" But with plenty of fists and fury, God cast
him down to the earth with you and me.
Yes, He cast him down to the earth with us,
yes, down to His earthly ground.
Okay, you've read what I just said, so tell me who
would you think was good and who was bad?
And Also Answer My Question of "Who
Cast Who Down?" As I First Asked.

***By** Jehovah* THROUGH THE HEART, MIND,
AND LEFT HAND OF ***Kevin Moss***

> And the great dragon was cast out, that old serpent, called the Devil, and Satan, which deceiveth the whole world: he was cast out into the earth, and his angels were cast out with him.
> —REVELATION 12:9

OKAY, NOW I'M THROUGH, SO AGAIN TELL ME, WHO WOULD YOU SAY CAST DOWN WHO?

Walking on Water

You know, walking on *water* is just one amazing thing
to do, and as Jesus Christ did it, we can too, true?
Now I know at times it may seem impossible,
but believe me, it can be done too!
Yes, it can, by both me and you.
Now walking on water is like you were standing in line at the
Grocery Store and one day someone accidentally bumped into you.
But they didn't say "I'm sorry" or "Excuse me, Sir."
No, they just looked at you wrongly and said,
"You better get out of my way!"
But you decide to walk on *water* by being the bigger one and
replying with a "Oh, I'm sorry, Sir, please forgive me, I do say."
And then you ended it with a "And have a nice day, Sir, Okay?"
Now you being the bigger man is like walking
on water for you just walked away.
Yes, I believe that's walking on water, wouldn't you say?
For walking on water is like turning the other cheek, so
be the bigger one and do as Jesus Christ, I must say.
Yes, just walk on water by being the bigger one, by just walking away.
Now I know it can be hard out here in this world sometimes
these days, and God knows it too, wouldn't you say?
And it's even harder being the bigger one at
times, yes, the one that walks away.
Yes, by just walking away from all kinds of
arguments and fights, I must say.
But please don't be like Peter and start sinking
in the water by the lack of faith.
For believe me, if you do, you're sure to drown in life today.
So don't do that, no, but be the strong one like Jesus and turn the
other cheek, and you'll then be walking on *water* truly, I must say.
And always remember that walking on water is just
turning the other cheek, turning the other cheek, yes,
turning the other cheek and just walking away.

Yes, humble yourself and let God into your life to change your whole rhythm and beat, alright?

By *Jehovah* THROUGH THE HEART, MIND, AND LEFT HAND OF ***Kevin Moss***

Be ye strong therefore, and let not your hands be weak; for your work will be rewarded.
—2 CHRONICLES 15:7

He That's First Will Be Last and He on the Top Will Be on the Bottom

There's so many in the world today that live for, and by,
nothing but material things, would not you say?
Yes, they live for material things, which are things of no life,
and they live for them every day in every way, I'd say!
Materials like US currency, which starts off being nothing
but a tree with life, yes, a tree, and nothing else but a tree!
But then the tree is made into shredded wood and later it's made
into paper, and with paper, they make things like US currency.
And we have so many today with lots of currency that think
about nothing else and no one else but themselves and money.
Now they put themselves first, but they're sure to see that in
the eyes of God, in the last days, they won't be first but last.
Yes, these kinds of people think they're first and also think that
they're on top, and at the moment, on top they pretty much are.
But believe me, these kinds of people will surely end up on the
bottom, the bottom, yes, the bottom, no fooling around.
Remember, Jesus did say a rich man getting to heaven is
like trying to get a camel through the eye of a needle.
And if you ask me, that's something that truly is impossible, and it
will never happen, which truly means one thing and one thing only.
AND THAT IS,
HE THAT'S FIRST WILL BE LAST and HE ON
THE TOP WILL BE ON THE BOTTOM!

***By** Jehovah* THROUGH THE HEART, MIND,
AND LEFT HAND OF ***Kevin Moss***

Because the foolishness of God is wiser then man, and the weakness of God is stronger then men.

—1 CORINTHIANS 1:25

Every Stone Shall Fall

Do you really know what Jesus meant when
He said every stone shall fall?
Now please believe me, everyone, for this He did once say, yes,
and He did say it for a reason, and He was talking to us all.
And what He meant by it was that one day, every building
and everything that man has built would truly, truly fall.
But He also meant us too, yes, both me and
you, one day will truly fall too.
Yes, everyone of us, meaning all, all, and all, again both me and you!
See, we all are spirit like God, our Heavenly Father, He that gave
life to all human beings, yes, all, all, and all, you know what I mean?
But while we're still alive in the flesh living on God's
earth in the flesh, which is our temple, which is
just another building, that also must fall.
Yes, He meant our human bodies too, when He
said to we all every building will fall.
Once again, He meant all, all, and all.
Yes, He Was Talking to We All the World When
He Said, "Every Stone Shall Fall."
I end by advising everyone again we all, all, and all to get ourselves
right with God through Jesus Christ for today you may just fall.
Believe Me, Just One More Time, When I Say
Once Again He Did Mean Us All.
Yes, He Meant Us All When He Said So Loud
and Clear That Every Stone Shall Fall!

By *Jehovah* THROUGH THE HEART, MIND,
AND LEFT HAND OF ***Kevin Moss***

The "outward man" is the earthen vessel (2 CORINTHIANS 4:7), the human body (2 CORINTHIANS 4:10), the mortal flesh (2 CORINTHIANS 4:11), and the earthly house (2 CORINTHIANS 5:1).

Therefore I hated life; because the work that is wrought under the sun is grievous unto me: for all is vanity and vexation of spirit. Yea, I hated all my labour which I had taken under the sun: because I should leave it unto the man that shall be after me.

—ECCLESIASTES 2:17–18

Don't False Teach My Children

The children of today are our world tomorrow, so where will
we be tomorrow if today, instead of love, we keep teaching the
children about things like guns and hate but not love?
Besides, didn't God say "Thou Shall Not Kill?" Yes,
He did, and even though it started out just His,
It's also come with love to also be my will.
And as the Father from high up above, I also will
that instead of hate, we learn to teach our children,
children, and our children's children
Love, Love, and more Love with Love, Love, and more Love!
Don't False Teach My Children; You're Better Off to Put a Chain
Around Your Neck and Throw Your Self in the Depths of the Sea!
Remember, we all were there once; that's right,
you too were once a sweet little child!
Now at that time, what did you like the most?
Yes, tell me, was it being teased, hollered, and screamed at or
being beat with hate? Boy, oh boy, I know that wasn't great!
But again tell me, was it not always having the soft feeling of
Mom's loving touch that was always there with love and not hate?
So please, as you were so loved, show the
same love to the children of today!
And teach them truth, with the same sweet love and not hate, okay?
NO, DON'T FALSE TEACH MY CHILDREN!
And Those Who Do, You're Better Off to Put a Chain Around
Your Neck and Throw Yourself in the Depths of the Sea.
REMEMBER, A CHILD IS BORN WITH
A GOLDEN HEART, YOU SEE?

***By** Jehovah* THROUGH THE HEART, MIND,
AND LEFT HAND OF ***Kevin Moss***

Saving Someone

Brethren, if any of you do err from the truth, and one convert him; Let him know, that he which converteth the sinner from the error of his way shall save a soul from death, and shall hide a multitude of sins.

—JAMES 5:19–20

He's Always There

He, God our Creator, Is always there; that's
right, that's right, yes, that's right!
Believe me, Mr. Jehovah Love Is here, there,
and everywhere every day and night.
Now I'm not telling you this to put fear in your heart, no, I'm not.
For you should know He's watching everything we do both me and you.
Yes, He's watching and sees everything for He's always there.
Now you may think that you're slick and get
away with everything you do, right?
But let me tell you that no you're not, and
you don't, for you're always caught.
And if you thought you were right, I tell you
straight to your face, you're wrong.
And that's because He's always there on, on, and on!
Yes, He's always there watching everything
we do, yes, He the One who cares.
Yes, He's always there watching both me and you and everything we do.
Believe me, He Is just as true as the sun does shine in the day.
And just as bright that the moon and stars do shine in the night.
So whoever you are, always keep this in mind,
remembering He's there at all times.
Yes, remember that the Bright Shining Light Is always there.
And also remember that He's the One who put
It there for He really, really cares.
Believe me, He and only He does things like that,
so don't be scared; He's always there.
Yes, He's the Bright Shining Light That's
Always There with You to Share.
And Believe Me, He's Always There for He Really, Really Cares!

***By** Jehovah* THROUGH THE HEART, MIND,
AND LEFT HAND OF ***Kevin Moss***

And the Lord God formed man of the dust of the ground, and breathed into his nostrils the Breath of Life; and man became a living soul.

Genesis 2:7

The Eyes Of The Lord. Are In Every Place, Beholding The Evil And The Good.

—PROVERBS 15:3

All Must Forgive All

Forgiving one another is something we all must learn to do.
Yes, you forgive me, and I forgive you!
Sometimes it can be so hard to do, then other
times, you don't know what to do.
BUT AS GOD, ALL MUST FORGIVE ALL;
YES, WE MUST FORGIVE ALL TOO.
And we must forgive from both the heart and the mind, TRUE?
Which means if you've truly forgiven someone,
You don't keep going back to the past, dwelling
on it time and time again, my friends!
No, don't do that, for once again we're to forgive
from both the heart and the mind.
AND ALWAYS REMEMBER AND NEVER FORGET
THAT IF YOU DON'T FORGIVE THEM,
GOD WONT FORGIVE YOU!

***By** Jehovah* THROUGH THE HEART, MIND,
AND LEFT HAND OF ***Kevin Moss***

My brethren, have not the faith of our Lord Jesus Christ, the Lord of glory, with respect of persons. For if there come unto your assembly a man with a gold ring, in goodly apparel, and there come in also a poor man in a vile raiment; And ye have respect to him that weareth the gay clothing, and say unto him, Sit thou here in a good place; and say to the poor, Stand thou there, or sit here under the footstool: Are ye not then partial in yourselves, and are become judges of evil thoughts? Hearken, my beloved brethren, *Hath not God chosen the poor of this world rich in faith, and heirs of the kingdom which He has promised to them that love Him?* But ye have despised the poor. Do not rich men oppress you, and draw you before the judgement seats? Do not they blaspheme that worthy name by which ye are called? If ye fulfill the royal law according to the scripture, *THOU SHALT LOVE THY NEIGHBOR AS THYSELF* ye do well:

But if ye have respect to persons, ye commit sin, and are convinced of the law as transgressors.

For whosoever shall keep the whole law, and yet offend in one point, he is guilty of all. For He that said, Do Not Commit no adultery, said also, Do Not Kill. Now if thou commit no adultery, yet if thou kill, thou art become a transgressor of the law.

—JAMES 2:1–11 (emphasis added)

Time Goes On

Time does go on, for time is one thing man just can't stop.
Yes, time does go on, and believe me, when I
say time is controlled from the top.
So always keep your head to the sky up to He,
and always believe His word to be.
Now man may have at the time some of our lives kind of looked up.
But still time is one thing he just can't stop!
No man can't stop time no matter how hard he tries.
So always keep your head, heart, and mind up, up, up high to the sky!
Yes, time goes on, and it already has been set;
yes, God has set both times, bet!
Yes, He's set both the time of our lives and the
time of our death oh yes, yes, yes.
Yes, He's set both the time of our birth and
the time of our death, you got that?
And believe me, when it comes to your time
and your number is called, you'll go.
Really, no one but He can give you more or give you less, do not you see?
So here on earth we shall remain until that very day!
Now could that be made any more plainer to, you would you say?
No, no plainer could I make it that God's the controller of time.
No matter how it's put, your time has already
been set, but are you ready to go yet?
Yes, believe me, all births and deaths were set by God the Father,
God the Son, and God the Holy Ghost that One, One, One!
So may we all repent today and not wait too long,
but with love, start singing a new song, called
always remembering in our hearts that
TIME GOES ON, ON, AND ON!

By *Jehovah* THROUGH THE HEART, MIND,
AND LEFT HAND OF ***Kevin Moss***

Verily, verily, I say unto you, The hour is coming, and now is, when the dead shall hear the voice of the Son of God: and they that hear shall live.

—JOHN 5:25

A Beautiful Flower

When I glance at your beautiful face, believe me, I truly see
such a beautiful flower glowing through God's loving grace.
Yes, I truly Believe that God does shine His light through you,
Another of His beautiful flowers!
I'm just another son of His, yes, one of His farmers
who's looking for a beautiful flower like you to
plant in my flower pot, which is my heart.
But It seems I've had a problem in finding such a flower as you to plant.
Yes, one that's as beautiful as you, because of Satan's hate,
I guess because I'm another child of God's, it happened to me as
it's happened to all His other children, for me too does Satan hate.
Yes, it seems to me when it comes to finding a
true friend to make my right arm.
I've truly been blocked, just blocked from a dream come true!
And that dream that I've been blocked from and wish to come
true is planting a beautiful flower in my heart like you.
Yes, I'd just love to plant you in my flowerpot.
And believe me, if I could, I'd just water you down with my love.
And to me, It's so true that all beautiful
flowers are God's sparks of love!
Yes, believe me, my love, I'd just do nothing but water you
down with my Love as God has watered us down with His.
And such a beautiful flower as Yourself would be so pleasing to care for.
Plus, love is even more powerful than water.
For as water gives life to a plant, feeding it to grow, our Love
for each other would do the same, yes, just grow, grow, grow.
Plus we'd then have one to talk and laugh with.
And when down, we'd have each other's shoulder to cry on, you know?
And true friends are Like two equaling one!
For 1, It takes both the dirt and the seed to plant a flower, and
2, It also takes the sun and the rain to help that flower to grow.
Yes, two, as Me and You!
For as the dirt, seed and the sun and rain have always been friends,

We would be friends too, again, again, and
again, yes, both Me and You, true?
Yes, friends we'd always be with true Love, and just like a flower,
our Love and Friendship would nothing but grow, grow, grow.
So forever may God, our Heavenly Father, shine
His Light down on both me and you as He does
all His other beautiful flowers with Love!

By Jehovah THROUGH THE HEART, MIND,
AND LEFT HAND OF ***Kevin Moss***

And the Lord God said, it is not good that man should be alone; I will make him an help mate for him.

—GENESIS 2:18

And the Lord God caused a deep sleep to fall on Adam, and he slept: and He took one of his ribs, and closed up the flesh instead thereof; And the rib, which the Lord God had taken from man, made He a woman, and brought her unto the man. And Adam said this is now bone of my bones, and flesh of my flesh: she shall be called Woman, because she was taken out of Man.

—GENESIS 2:21–23

Yield, Stop, and Go!

Hey there, world, would you yield for a moment
and dig this before you make another move?
I believe that we the world really need to yield for a moment or
two and realize just what time it is we're now living in, you know?
And yes, that means both me and you!
Now just yield and take a look around at the pain so many families
are going through because of hate, and also the Climate Change.
In other words, you know it's really getting hot
out here today, if you know what I mean!
I know one thing man needs to do is stop, yes, stop, all the
hate he shows hurting and killing others before it's too late.
Yes, that's surely one thing we all need to do!
Now with Love, Love, and more Love, let's all go, go, go and
just show to all Love, Love, and more Love, you know?
Stop looking away from God, but look to He, for
believe me, whatever our problem may be, He
can and will solve it for every one of we.
Please stop fearing God, but take your problems to God for
God's the problem solver and is truly the Father for all of we.
So go and repent to Jesus Christ right now for God said if you
accept My Son as your Savior, I'll accept you as My Own child!
And at any time, He will, whether it be day or night,
He will, so Go, Go, Go, yes, Go, Go, Go, alright?

***By** Jehovah* THROUGH THE HEART, MIND,
AND LEFT HAND OF ***Kevin Moss***

Awake, O sword, against my shepherd, and against the man that is my fellow, saith the Lord of hosts: smite the shepherd, and the sheep shall be scattered: and I will turn My hand upon the little ones.

—ZECHARIAH 13:7

May We Learn to Blow Out Angels of Love

Would you not say it would be so much better if we
blew out of our mouths Angels, yes, Love?
Yes, if we blew out Angels instead of hate
and Angels instead of threats,
Well, I would, for then would we have a
much better world to live in.
Yes, that would be just so great for it wouldn't
be a loss but would surely be a win.
But it seems in this world we live in today, there's
more Demons blown out than Angels,
Which means more Hate than Love!
I also want all to know that Demons are of Satan from hell below
and Angels come from God of the heavens high above, with Love!
On top of that, what comes out the mouth first comes
from the heart and mind and surely not the back.
So I end saying what I thought and said from the start, which
was "May we all learn to blow out a lot more Angels of Love."
FOR ANGELS, ANGELS, YES, ANGELS OF
PURE, PURE LOVE COME FROM THE HEART
WITH LOVE, LOVE, AND MORE LOVE!

***By** Jehovah* THROUGH THE HEART, MIND,
AND LEFT HAND OF ***Kevin Moss***

Honest Wages

Go to now, ye rich men, weep and howl for your miseries that shall come upon you. Your riches are corrupted, and your garments are moth-eaten. Your gold and silver is cankered; and the rust of them shall be a witness against you, and shall eat your flesh as it were fire. Ye have heaped treasure together for the last days. Behold, the hire of the labourers who have reaped down your fields, which is of you kept back by fraud, crieth: and the cries of them which have reaped are entered into the ears of the Lord of Sabbath.

—JAMES 5:1–4

The Love of Jesus Christ Day and Night

The Love of Jesus Christ is so, so good and oh so bright!
I guess for starters, that's because He first gave His life with Love,
and through His were we given the chance to get back ours, right?
And believe me, truly His Love shines brighter than the sun of the
day, which is far more brighter than the moon and stars at night.
His Love is so soft and oh so bright that it feels like a nice, cool
breeze blowing a kite of Love through our lives every day and night,
Which means today the best move you could ever make is picking
up your cross with Love and following He, Jesus Christ.
Believe me, for what I tell you, I tell you with nothing
but Love, and that's telling you that letting the Holy
Spirit lead you is nothing else but right.
And great for you it'll be, for you'll then be taking your life
out of check and at the same time telling Satan checkmate.
And everyone should know the one that says "checkmate" has
won the game, and the game you've won is life, early, not late.
Yes, you've truly won the game of life, and
you won it so free, easy, and nice.
For you won this game through the Love and
Blood of our Lord, Jesus Christ!

***By** Jehovah* THROUGH THE HEART, MIND,
AND LEFT HAND OF ***Kevin Moss***

And now, O Lord my God, thou hast made thy servant King instead of David my father: and I'm a little child: I know not how to go out or come in.

—1 KINGS 3:7

Happiness, Peace, and Joy Is God the Greatest

True, happiness only God can give to you, and He will, yes, He
will believe me, He will, if you'll first do His will, He will!
Yes, He'll tell you in your heart that you've just been
given a true lifetime deal, if you'll just do His will.
Peace is just so Kind, Gentle, and Soft, you know?
It's Peace with Love I'd truly like to see, and it's also where I'd like
to be, yes, in a world filled with Love, Happiness, Peace, and Joy.
Do you know that Love is the key of life and that
Love is the strongest force we have, yes, it is for Love is
Jehovah, God the Father—Jesus Christ, God the Son,
and God the Comforting, Holy Ghost, right!
HAPPINESS, PEACE, AND JOY IS GOD WITH
LOVE, LOVE, AND MORE LOVE WHO'S
JUST THE GREATEST, ALRIGHT?
Such a joy it truly is when you know you're
Loved both day and night.
And Loved we truly are by God who said, "When You Thought
There Was No Love, There Was, For I Loved You First."
God's Love stretches from He the Best down to we the Worst,
and believe me, God does Love us all with a Great Big BURST.
Now let your Love go out into the world with
that exact same burst, for it's not too late.
And believe me, if you do, God will let His Happiness,
Peace, and Joy just flow through both me and you.
Now Don't Wait Too Long and End Up Being Late,
for to God, That Wouldn't Be Very Great.
BUT ALWAYS REMEMBER, HAPPINESS, PEACE, AND
JOY ARE GOD'S, WHO'S JUST THE GREATEST!

***By** Jehovah* THROUGH THE HEART, MIND,
AND LEFT HAND OF ***Kevin Moss***

And besides this, giving all diligence, add to your faith virtue; and to virtue knowledge; And to knowledge temperance; and to temperance patience; and to patience Godliness; And to Godliness brotherly kindness; and to brotherly kindness charity. For if these things be in you, and abound, they make you that ye shall neither be barren nor unfruitful in the knowledge of our Lord Jesus Christ. But he that lacketh these things is blind, and cannot see afar off, and hath forgotten that he was purged from his old sins. Wherefore the rather, brethren, give diligence to make your calling and election sure: for if ye do these things, ye shall never fall: For so an entrance shall be ministered unto you abundantly into the everlasting kingdom of our Lord and Saviour Jesus Christ.

—2 PETER 1:5–11

The New Heaven Earth

I'm sure Heaven is nothing else but beautiful, for
it's the home of our Lord, Jesus Christ.
It's a planet that's so full of Love, Love, and more Love, and there
it's just bright, bright, bright, for remember there, God is the Light.
It will brighten your life with love; yes, true
love will truly brighten your life.
For love is God with our Lord, Jesus Christ.
For in heaven, there's nothing else but Love, Love,
and more Love; yes, it's truly, truly alright?
But it seems here today on earth, we have more hate than Love,
am not I right? Yes, we do, so what happened to the light?
Well, He went back home to heaven and now sits at His Father's right.
But He'll soon be coming back with Love for again Love is Jesus Christ.
Now in case you didn't get it, it goes as so, on the
New Planet Earth coming back with Him, Hate,
Anger, Hurt, and Pain won't exist then!
BUT WHY?
Because they will also be cast down to hell right along with sin.
And then a new day with a new life for us all will surely begin.
Yes, it will indeed for then Love, Love, and more Love will truly be
back in whole once again, all my brothers, sisters, and friends. Yes,
when Jesus Christ our Lord, Savior, and King comes back, He'll
be bringing with Him with a great big burst on His right side.
"THE NEW HEAVEN EARTH!"

***By** Jehovah* THROUGH THE HEART, MIND,
AND LEFT HAND OF ***Kevin Moss***

And the gates of it shall not be shut at all by day: for there shall be no night there. And they shall bring the glory and honor of the nations into it. And there shall in no wise enter into it anything that defileth, neither whatsoever worketh abomination, or maketh a lie: but they which are written in the Lamb's book of life.

—REVELATIONS 21:25–27

The Meaning of Happiness, Peace, and Joy

HAPPINESS, happiness is like waking up in the
morning with a smile on your face every single day.
It's like knowing in your heart with faith that
everything's going to be OKAY.
Which is like the day He comes back to reclaim what
is His; oh what a day, what a day, what a day!
Yes, that's going to be one happy, happy day, would not you say?
PEACE: peace is like a gentle feeling of comfort with no worry at all.
No, you'll have no worry, for with faith, you know in your
heart that Jesus Christ will be there at your every call.
It's such a peaceful feeling when God blows His Love through our
lives like a nice, cool breeze; yes, does He blow it through us all.
Yes, every single day God blows His pure Love through us all.
Yes, He does, whether it's winter, summer, spring, or fall.
Peace, peace, peace, yes, I just Love Happiness
and Peace with a nice touch of Joy.
JOY: joy is like a child jumping up and down with
happiness and peace after just getting a brand-new toy.
Or it can be like another happy Christmas
where, with peace, you do celebrate.
Yes, you do with your family and friends with joy, joy, and more joy.
For, yes, it's such a joy laughing with your family and friends
in true happiness, peace with joy, oh boy, oh boy, oh boy.
For to you, you're one, as God the Father, God the Holy
Ghost, and Jesus Christ, God the Son are One!
Now whether the Three, One at the moment, are in the
form of the Father, Son, or Holy Ghost doesn't matter.
For Happiness, Peace, and Joy still is that very
special One that we all Love the most.
SO TOO HAPPINESS, PEACE, AND JOY
WITH LOVE, LOVE, AND MORE LOVE. LET
US all MAKE A GREAT BIG TOAST!

By Jehovah THROUGH THE HEART, MIND, AND LEFT HAND OF ***Kevin Moss***

Simon Peter, a servant and an apostle of Jesus Christ, to them that have obtained like precious faith with us through the righteousness of God and our Saviour Jesus Christ: Grace and peace be multiplied unto you through the knowledge of God, and of Jesus our Lord, According as His divine power hath given unto us all things, that pertain unto life and Godliness, through the knowledge of Him that hath called us to glory and virtue: Whereby are given unto us exceeding great and precious promises: that by these ye might be partakers of the divine nature, having escaped the corruption that is in the world through lust.

—2 PETER 1:1–4

Such a Lovely Friend

You know what?
I think I met one today, yes, one true and Lovely friend I'd say.
And a lovely friend is someone I pray to God for every single day.
I guess that's because a lovely friend is someone
that will make another's day oh so gay.
And believe me, a lovely friend is someone needed by we
all, for at times we all have days that can be so hard!
Yes, at times, one's day can be Just oh so hard from beginning to end.
And then from end to the beginning all over again.
Now I believe it's times like this that the best thing
one could have is a lovely, lovely friend.
For a true friend is one that cares about every
tear that drops from the eyes of another.
Believe me, one like this is such a lovely friend, such a lovely friend.
And they're such a lovely friend again, again, and again!
But it seems today a true friend is someone
very hard to find, I must say!
Now I guess that's because we're living in a time and
age that most of the world only have one care.
Yes, only one care, their self, and their own
wants and needs, what just isn't fair.
And God nor myself believes that this is the
way we're supposed to be, Okay?
For Loving, Caring or Giving, Sweetness, kindness by Helping
others is God, and that's Who and the Way we're to be.
Yes, we're to be this way to the very, very end, for
then would we be like God the Father, God the
Son, and God the Holy Ghost, friends.
For then we'd all be such a lovely friend, such
a lovely friend yes, a lovely friend!
And that's someone I wish I could call
everyone, yes, such a Lovely Friend.

By** Jehovah* THROUGH THE HEART, MIND, AND LEFT HAND OF ***Kevin Moss

A friend liveth at all times, and a brother is born for adversity?

—PROVERBS 17:17

Just One

One, yes, 1 Is a number that you're about
to see; is a big 1, not a small one.
And that's for several different reasons and not just 1.
For instance, think about all the different animals we have in the
world today, and I'm sure you know there's a lot more than one.
And every one of them is an animal of some kind, and not just 1.
For remember even man, yes, man is considered
an animal; yes, we too are one.
On top of that, at times some human beings even
act like animals or beasts, but just some.
But all animals, no matter what kind of animal
they are, were still given life by God.
That's God the Father, God the Son, and God the Holy Ghost,
where we have three different forms, but They're still only ONE.
Now it's from that One that we're given the family
of the fowl, the mammal, and also the beast.
"BUT HOW?"
Because God, Mr. Life Himself, gave life to us all;
yes, to we the most, but also to them the least.
And let us not forget the family of the plant, the insect, and the
reptile or any other family that exist for remember, God made us all.
And believe me, this means that we all do come together; no
matter what Race, creed, or Color, we're all sisters and brothers!
Yes, we all come together for everything of life was given life by
1 God, and there's only *One* God, and we're all creations of *He.*
And I guess that means even though we're all different types of
animals, we're still one family, so together we all do comc!
YES, WE'RE all JUST 1. AS GOD THE FATHER,
GOD THE HOLY GHOST, AND ALSO GOD
THE SON, WE TOO ARE ONE.
"JUST ONE, WE'RE A BIG 1. BUT STILL JUST ONE!"

By *Jehovah* THROUGH THE HEART, MIND, AND LEFT HAND OF ***Kevin Moss***

What shall we say then? Shall we continue in sin, that grace may abound? God forbid. How shall we that are dead to sin, live any longer therein? Know ye not, that so many of us were baptized into Jesus Christ were baptized into His death?

—ROMANS 6:1–3

With Love May We Kiss Again, Again, and Again

Yes, with love, my children may we kiss again, again, and
again for it's so true that I'm yours and you're mine.
And with love may we always be each others
with the same love at all times.
Believe me, my children, each one of you, through
the Love of God, was given life.
And He allowed me, your mother, to deliver you into this
world, and I did with nothing else but Love, alright.
For this reason alone, I ask you, my children, with
Love, may we kiss again, again, and again?
Now it was because of Love, my daughter, that not very long ago
me and your brother both were so afraid that we'd lose you.
Yes, we were afraid we'd lose both you and your Love
And would never see you again.
But through the Love, Grace, and Power of God with the
Blood of Jesus Christ and the power of prayer, we didn't.
Believe me, my Love, with real Love so much did we care and
with the same Love, I'm so grateful that with us, you're still here.
And Through LOVE, With LOVE, and for LOVE, I Once Again
Say to You, My Children, You're Truly My Everlasting Friends!
So with love, love, pure love, I say, with LOVE, may
WE ALL KISS AGAIN, AGAIN, AND AGAIN?

***By** Jehovah* THROUGH THE HEART, MIND,
AND LEFT HAND OF ***Kevin Moss***

Wherefore I will not be negligent to put you always in remembrance of these things, though ye know them, and be established, in the present truth. Yea, I think it meet, as long as I am in this tabernacle, to stir you up by putting you in remembrance; Knowing that shortly I must put off this my tabernacle, even as our Lord Jesus Christ hath shewed, me. Moreover I will endeavour that ye may be able after my decease to have these things always in remembrance,—death.

—2 PETER 1:12–15

We Must, We Must, We Must!

I truly do believe that we all wish to get to heaven one day.
I also know that we all won't, but God did make a way for
us, and He goes by the name of Jesus Christ, Okay?
Now truly do we all want peace in our lives every single day,
which comes with happiness and joy in every little way.
And truly we all can have it in our lives with
pure, pure love in every little way.
But we first must do what God said was to be done, just
as it was first done by Jesus Christ, God's first Son.
I also believe that some wish and also pray that their
name will be in the Book of Life one day.
For then would they live in heaven with God the Father, Jesus
Christ, God the Son, and God the Holy Ghost as One.
But once again may we all remember that first we must follow
the footprints of Jesus Christ up that narrow path, do I say.
Yes, that's right, we all must do what Jesus has already done.
BUT HOW?
By just doing what was earlier said, and this we must do as one.
YES, WE MUST, WE MUST, WE MUST!
We must all do what God said was to be done,
and again we must do it as one.
And that's doing His will by following His laws as it
was first done by Jesus Christ, His first Son.

***By** Jehovah* THROUGH THE HEART, MIND,
AND LEFT HAND OF ***Kevin Moss***

Forasmuch then as Christ hath suffered for us in the flesh, arm yourselves likewise with the same mind: for He that hath suffered in the flesh hath ceased from sin; That he no longer should live the rest of his time in the flesh to the lusts of men, but to the will of God.

—1 PETER 4:1–2

My Word Shall Always Stand

And God spoke all these words, saying, "I am the Lord, thy God."
But it seemed that we the world, for some
reason, didn't believe, but why?
I mean, after all, He's created and done for us, shouldn't
He have our praise and glory without all the fuss?
On top of that, don't forget as well as Him giving us His
commands, He also said to we the world very clearly,
"MY WORD SHALL ALWAYS STAND!"
Now let us take a walk back into Noah's time and age, a time
when just about all human beings had lost their mind.
Yes, all but one man three sons and four wives!
And I guess that was because it seemed in that time and age,
man didn't want to listen to anything that God had to say.
Now the funny thing about that is, it seems that we the
world are today thinking and acting the exact same way.
For instance, do you remember in the Bible where
God told Noah to build the ark on land?
Then I'm sure you also remember how the world laughed
at him for choosing to follow God's commands.
After that, the next thing you know was Noah
and his family were floating away.
And just for that reason alone, if you ask me,
Noah had the last laugh, wouldn't you say?
Now after all that has happened, I'd say the first thing to
remember is that there's only one God, if you ask me.
And believe me, it's He that's the First Man, and please,
let not anyone forget what it was that He said!
Yes, when He once said those most powerful words to all mankind!
And yes, I tell you all once again that He meant everything He
said, yes, when it was said to us all by He, the First MAN.
MY WORD SHALL ALWAYS STAND!

By *Jehovah* THROUGH THE HEART, MIND, AND LEFT HAND OF ***Kevin Moss***

By faith Noah, being warned of God of things not seen as yet, moved with fear, prepare an ark to the saving of his house; by the which he condemned the world, and became heir of the righteousness which is by faith.

—HEBREWS 11:7

I Will to Do His Will

I will to do His will, yes, the will of God above, and the first
thing He wills us all to do is spread, yes, spread His Love.
So show pure love to everyone as if everyone were He;
yes, I show love to you, and you show love to me.
And let us all do His will, which is showing love to all;
yes, loving all is God's will, don't you hear His call?
Is it such a hard, hard thing to do, yes, showing love to all?
No, it really isn't, so treat everyone with love, like everyone were
your own Mother, Father, Sister, and Brother, for love does call all.
Remember, God so loved we the world that just for us, He gave
the life of His only begotten Son; yes, His Son He did call.
And the Son so loved the Father, and we the world that His
life He did willingly give for nothing else but love you-al.
Yes, for us, He gave His life with nothing else but love; yes, it
was He that gave us life with Love, Love, and more Love.
And if you ask me, that makes Him number one, so if there's
anyone to follow, it's Jesus Christ, yes, God's first Son.
Yes, My Heavenly Father, I Will to Do Your
Will; I Pray It Will Be Done!
This I do, I do, I do for I became a child of God when God
adopted me, and with love do I say He'll also adopt you too.
Yes, you can become a child of God for His offer is to all,
and God will be there with love for you at your every call.
For God, our Heavenly Father, is just full, full, yes, full of nothing
else but Love; yes, He's just so full of Love, Love, and more Love.
So believe me, everyone, it's really not hard being forgiven of all
our sins; in fact, it's pretty easy and it's not a loss but truly is a win.
Yes, you-al, ask for forgiveness by repenting of
your sins, and His blood will wash you clean,
and your life He'll change scene by scene.
I WILL TO DO HIS WILL; YES, LET HIS WILL BE DONE!

By** Jehovah* THROUGH THE HEART, MIND, AND LEFT HAND OF ***Kevin Moss

Then Paul answered, What mean ye to weep and to break my heart? For I am ready not to be bound only, but also to die at Jerusalem for the name of the Lord Jesus.

—ACTS 21:13

Through Love and Faith We Sail

For the love that our God had for us then, did He give the
life of His first Son, *Emmanuel.* Amen, Amen, Amen.
And by doing so, with love, He provided a way for we sinners to win.
And by just having faith, believing in He, by spirit you can be born
again, and believe me, being born again is the only way to win.
Yes, it is for Jesus Christ, who's truly God's first
Son, has for we the world already won.
So let's all sing with joy, with joy, with joy as we sail, singing a new
song right along with the ringing in our hearts, yes, our glory bells.
For through love and faith and being spiritually revived, we've
become another child of God's, so we do sail high in the sky.
Now as our Lord Jesus Christ told His first Disciples what they
must do, we, Disciples of His, must do the same thing too.
Yes, we must also go out into the world, providing whatever is
necessary in helping others to spread His Love and Word, as well.
We're to help convince the unsaved how important it is to be saved,
for we're so close to the end of sin, followed by the New Beginning.
Our job is to spread God's Love and His Word,
yes, being fruitful and multiplying by helping to
convince the unsaved to become saved.
Yes, we're to convince them that as it was once
before, it shall be again, and this time, it shall be
eternal, yes, forever and ever, my friends.
And believe me, you-al, then the body of Jesus Christ, the first and
true Vessel, will soon be coming back down to get what is His.
Again believe me, for we're about at that point now when the Vessel,
again the true body of Christ, will truly be coming back down.
So we must help as many as we can to repent, for only true believers
will be on this vessel going up to heaven and not down to hell.
YES, THE TRUE BODY OF CHRIST SHALL SOON,
FROM THIS EARTH, BE MAKING ITS LAST SAIL!

By** Jehovah* THROUGH THE HEART, MIND, AND LEFT HAND OF ***Kevin Moss

For Christ also hath once suffered for sins, the just for unjust, that He might bring us to God, being put to death in the flesh, but quickened, by the Spirit.

—1 PETER 3:18

Two but One

Well, Merry, Merry Christmas, Sis, and Happy, Happy New Year!
Now you may not believe me, but I do wish you many, many more,
for here you have a brother that loves you and really, really cares.
Yes, I do love you, and when it comes to you, I also really care.
Please believe me, my sister, for I'm sure you
know I love you more than none!
Yes, I really do love you, for even though we're
two, believe me, still we're only one.
Yes, we are my Sister, for you're the Daughter and I'm the Son,
but since we're twins, even though we're two, still we're only one.
Now I know when we were children, we had our ups
and downs and our ins and outs while growing up.
You know, all those times when you'd scratch me
like a cat and I'd squeeze you like a bear.
But, my dear loving sister, I'm sorry, but I'm afraid
we've grown up now and aren't children anymore.
So to you, yes, you my sister, whom I really, really love, do I
wish you a Merry, Merry Christmas and a Happy New Year.
And I want you to know just how much I really
do miss you, and with love, I also want you to
know that you really have nothing to fear!
Don't, for it will always be the same sweet love.
So don't ever forget that I'm still here.
Yes, Truly We're Two, but Through Love,
We'll Always Be One, My Dear!

***By** Jehovah* THROUGH THE HEART, MIND,
AND LEFT HAND OF ***Kevin Moss***

And Esau ran to meet him, and embraced him, and fell on his neck, and kissed him: and then wept.

—GENESIS 33:4

Did You Thank the Lord?

Did you thank the Lord today?
Did you thank the Lord, did you thank the
Lord, I said, did you thank the Lord?
For we should all be thanking He, that's right, both you and me!
Yes, we should be thanking Him for the Heavens, thanking
Him for the Earth and thanking Him for the Great Blue Sea.
That's right, thank Him for all life right along with me!
Now Did You Thank the Lord, Did You Thank
the Lord Again, Did You Thank the Lord?
Every day we must thank God for our Lord, Jesus Christ,
who died on the cross to give us back life; yes, He paid
the cost, yes, He paid the right price "LIFE."
SO DID YOU THANK THE LORD?
Well, thank Him, thank Him, thank Him, and
thank Him again, again, and again!
Yes, thank Him for the Holy Ghost, who's no one else
but God Himself, yes, He the Host of Hosts.
And He's the most, for the Holy Ghost is how
He puts Himself into you and me both.
So everyone thank Him for as I've written God
is nothing but the true, true HOST!
TRUE?

***By** Jehovah* THROUGH THE HEART, MIND,
AND LEFT HAND OF ***Kevin Moss***

And I beheld, and heard the voice of many Angels round about the throne and the beast and the elders: and the number of them was ten thousand times thousand, and thousand of thousands.
—REVELATION 5:11

NOW WOULD YOU THANK THE LORD?

Thanks for Another Day

I thank You, Lord, I thank You, yes, I thank You, for the air that
I breathe, and I thank You, my Lord, for the food that I eat.
Yes, I thank You for You're the One that fulfills all my needs.
I thank You, Lord, for the bright shining sun; yes, I
thank You, my Heavenly Father, as should everyone.
Yes, I thank He who's God the Father, God the Son, and God
the Holy Ghost; yes, I thank You for another day, my Host.
I thank You for the moon in the night that
shines with the stars oh so bright.
I thank You, Father, for every single planet as the
Heavens above, the Earth beneath, and also for
Jupiter and Mars, do I thank You too.
Yes, I thank You, I thank You, I thank You and Also Love
You with all my Heart, Mind, Body, and Soul.
And I thank You, King Jesus Christ, my Savior,
for You saved my life in whole.
I also thank You for every bird that flies and that walks, along
with every other animal and beast, the best and the least.
Yes, I Thank You, I Thank You, I Thank You Every Day in Peace!
I thank You for every fish that swims in the sea; yes,
for every single mammal do I thank Thee.
Believe me, my Heavenly Father, I thank You for every form of life,
and I end as I began by thanking You for another day and night.
Yes, Thank You, Thank You, Thank You. Thanking
You Is the Least That We Can Do.
You, my God, Father and Creator, my Lord, King, and Savior, who's
also my Brother and best, best Friend, I thank You for another day.
YES, I THANK YOU AGAIN, AGAIN, AND AGAIN
DO I THANK YOU FOR ANOTHER DAY.

***By** Jehovah* THROUGH THE HEART, MIND,
AND LEFT HAND OF ***Kevin Moss***

For if we have been planted together in the likeness of His death, we shall be also in the likeness of His resurrection: Knowing this, that our old man is crucified with Him, that the body of sin might be destroyed, that hence forth we should not serve sin. For he that is dead is freed from sin.

—ROMANS 6:5–7

The Heart and the Mind

The heart is a member of our human flesh for it pumps
blood through our bodies, which is a hell of a quest.
But we also have a spiritual heart that lets people
know just what kind of person we really are.
Yes, it clearly shows the inside of one; that's right, it shows whether
you're made of Vinegar or if you're the Honey kind of one.
Now the mind in your head shows one your intelligence; yes, by
your actions, it shows just how you think and also your fashion.
For instance, one that would blaspheme the Holy Spirit is one
I don't think is too smart and doesn't have a lot of passion.
No, I really wouldn't want to mix with someone
that would blaspheme the Holy Spirit; no, I don't
think I'd like to be at one of their sessions!
For remember, coming straight from He high
up above, it was said that blaspheme of the Holy
Spirit is something you can't be forgiven of!
Now do you understand that in your mind?
Well, just in case you don't, what I'm saying here is, things like
blaspheme of the Holy Spirit are controlled from the mind.
But in the Heart and Mind of God, it's Love that will always be,
and just like it's in Him, it should also always be in you and me.
Now you know that Love has always been in God's heart,
for He's shown us nothing but Love from the very start.
So May We all Just As He Make Love, Love, and More Love
Truly Be the First Mark in Both Our Mind and Our Heart.

***By** Jehovah* THROUGH THE HEART, MIND,
AND LEFT HAND OF ***Kevin Moss***

For what shall it profit a man, if he shall
gain the whole world., and lose his soul? Or what
shall a man give in exchange for his soul?
—MARK 8:36–37

Lost but Found

It feels so good when you realize that you are truly Loved, and we
are for we've had true Love sent down to us from high up above.
Now you may have been lost, but through the Love
of God, you can and may have also been found.
Yes, You Might Be Lost, but Through the Love and Blood of God,
Yes, Jesus Christ, Our Lord and Savior, You Can Be Found.
Oh yes, yes, yes, by the blood of Jesus are the lost saved, saved, yes,
saved; and by the blood of Christ are they found, found, found.
But still it hurts in this life we live to feel lost,
but unfortunately, sometimes we are.
But to be found by Love with Faith, we're just hoping, hoping,
and hoping that He's always there and never loses His Grace.
And Also with Hope, Love, and Faith, always
remember what God said when He did Truly say.
Ask and You Shall Receive, Seek and You Shall
Find, Knock and the Door Shall Open!
Now so many times I, too, was lost, but through pure, pure Love,
I've been found, yes, found by Prayer, Hope with Love and Faith.
Believe me, at first, we're all lost, but if you just repent, you're then
washed clean by the Blood of Christ and are given back Eternal Life.
Yes, through the Love of God the Father and God the Son are
we found and given back life through God the Holy Ghost.
So you have not lost but have truly, truly won, won,
yes, won, as did Jesus Christ the first Son.
For in God do we find Love, Love, and more Love, and it's through
His strong LOVE that we may be lost but we can also be found.
For It Has Been Proven That Today So Many
OF Us Are Just Lost, Lost, Lost!
But It's Also Been Proven That Oh So Many Of
Us Have Been Found, Found, Found!

***By** Jehovah* THROUGH THE HEART, MIND,
AND LEFT HAND OF ***Kevin Moss***

Wherefore, as by one man sin entered, into the world, and death by sin; and so death passed upon all men, for that all have sinned: (For until the law sin was in the world: but sin is not imputed when there is no law. Nevertheless death reigned from Adam to Moses, even over them that had not sinned after the similitude of Adam's transgression, who is the figure of Him that was to come. But not as the offence, so is as the free gift. For if through the offence of one many be dead, much more the grace of God, and the gift by grace, which is by One Man, Jesus Christ, hath abounded unto many. And not as it was by one that had sinned, so is the gift: for the judgment was by one to condemnation, but the free gift is of many offences unto justification. For if by one mans offence death reigned by one; much more they which receive abundance of grace and the gift of righteousness shall reign in life by One, Jesus Christ.) Therefore as by the offence of one judgment came upon all men to condemnation; even so by the righteousness of One the free gift came upon all men unto justification of life. For as by one man's disobedience many were made sinners, so by the obedience of One shall many be made righteous. Moreover the law entered, that the offence might abound, grace did more abound: That as sin hath reigned unto death, even so might grace reign through righteousness unto eternal life by

"Jesus Christ Our Lord."

—Romans 5:12–21

The True Color of Love!

Love really does have so many different colors that truly do show.
But how, for Love only has One color that's so
bright that it shines as Bright as the Shining Light,
for bright is God Himself who is the Light.
Yes, Love, Love, and more Love is the true color of God, who with
happiness, peace, and joy, it's Love He blows in the wind, alright?
And if you believe that Love He's not, then just tell me why; okay,
we're waiting for an answer from you, so now you're on the spot.
Remember that first God made the heavens, where
truly sits His throne, then with the same exact Love,
He made the earth and made it our home, right?
And don't ever forget God made the whole entire sea; yes, He did,
and with the exact same Love, He made it all just for you and me.
Yes, it was He, Mr. Love, who made you, me, and just all of we;
yes, God made all of we and everything else of life that you see.
And God so Loved we the world that He sent
down from heaven His only begotten Son; that's
right, you got it, Jesus Christ is the One.
Believe me, all these wonderful things God has made
and done has so many beautiful, Loving colors.
But no matter what the color is or may have been,
it's God's Love coming from, all His promises to
us, all my brothers, sisters, and friends.

***By** Jehovah* THROUGH THE HEART, MIND,
AND LEFT HAND OF ***Kevin Moss***

And spared not the old world, but saved Noah the eighth person, a preacher of righteousness, bringing in the flood upon the world of the ungodly; And turning the cities of Sodom and Go-mor'-rha into ashes Condemned them with an overthrow, making them an ensemble unto those that after should live ungodly; And delivered just Lot, vexed with the filthy conversation of the wicked.

—2 PETER 2:5–7

A Manipulator

A Manipulator is someone like the operator of a
bulldozer, for with skill they operate a machine.
Yes, a machine that pushes and pulls the earth
we walk on all over itself on, on, and on.
Preparing the ground for the next foundation we'll be building on.
A Manipulator is also one like Satan who manipulated Eve in the
book of Genesis when he asked her the woman this question.
Hath God said, "Ye shall not eat of every tree in the garden?"
And the women replied in Genesis 3:3
to the serpent's question with,
"Of the tree in the midst of the garden God said ye shall
not eat of it, neither shall ye touch it, lest ye die."
But Satan manipulated her in Genesis
3:4–5 in the form of the serpent.
He lied to her, saying, "You shall not surely die: For God doth
know that in the day ye eat thereof, then your eyes shall be opened,
and ye be as gods, knowing good from evil."
A Manipulator is also One like Jesus Christ for not another will
use you for any better reason than He, the One that died for we.
And yes, He calls all of we, just like the Father first called He!
God used the King of Kings who's the Lord of
Lords and the Manipulator of Manipulators.
It was He who managed His disciples oh so
skillfully, and we, yes, you and me are to faithfully
believe in He with trust and love, you see?
And if all would just let Him in their lives, He would with
Love, Love, and more Love run their lives oh so skillfully!
Now I'm not trying to manipulate you when I say,
give your life back to He who first gave it to ye.
But always remember and never forget to never
try manipulating another one Satan's way.
Believe me, I'm not lying, for lying to a neighbor is wrong; it's also
like trying to manipulate you the wrong way, wouldn't you say?

By *Jehovah* THROUGH THE HEART, MIND, AND LEFT HAND OF ***Kevin Moss***

Now the serpent was more subtle than any beast of the field, which the Lord God had made. And he said unto the woman, Yea, hath God said, Ye shall not eat of every tree of the garden? And the women said unto the serpent, We may eat of the fruit of the trees of the garden: But of the fruit of the tree which is in the midst of the garden, God hath said, Ye shall not eat of it, neither shall ye touch it, lest ye die. And the serpent said unto the woman, Ye shall not surely die: For God doth know that in the day ye eat thereof, then your eyes shall be opened, and ye shall be as gods, knowing good and evil.

—GENESIS 3:1–5

First, Not Last

So many people today think it's much more important putting
games and world events and things of that nature first, not last.
And I must say, this is coming to be a problem for
way too many of us in the world today.
And it's one problem that we must change right away, which means
now, because time is running out and it's running out fast, okay?
Just take a look around you, and tell me, what do you see?
Well, it seems to me most people are still not putting God
first but are still putting Him last, if you ask me.
But the way things seem to be going today, we all best
start putting Him first and get out of His way, okay?
And to so many that ask the question "Why?" do I say because the
end which comes before the new begging isn't very far away, I'd say.
No, it truly isn't, and the way it's getting out here today makes it
feel like the earth is about ready to explode in every little way.
And believe me, it then would be merry on its way!
So first and not last is where we should be putting
God in our lives every day and in every way.
Now I know what He said when He said; I'll never change
the productivity of the earth ever again in any way.
What He meant was, He would never again destroy
every living thing on His earth by a flood, okay?
But the next time He's going to destroy it by fire and the heaven
and the earth will both melt, that's right, just melt away.
Yes, by the power of God, this earth we live on
will be burned up and truly melt away!
So please start putting God first and not last in your life, okay?

***By** Jehovah* THROUGH THE HEART, MIND,
AND LEFT HAND OF ***Kevin Moss***

But, the day of the Lord will come as a thief in the night; in the which the heavens shall pass away with a great noise, and the elements shall melt with fervent heat, the earth also and the works that are therein shall be burned up. Seeing then that all these things shall be dissolved, what manner of persons ought ye to be in all holy conversation and godliness. Looking for and hasting unto the coming of the day of God, wherein the heavens being on fire shall be dissolved, and the elements shall melt with fervent heat?

—2 Peter 3:10–11

Nothing's Free and Lasts Forever but God's Love

There's truly nothing in this world today that's free
and lasts forever but God's Love, if you ask me.
Now He first loved us oh so much that after creating the Heavens
and the Earth, He then created man from dirt yes, His earth.
Yes, God Loved man oh so much that after sin came
equaling death, He sent down from heaven His first
Son, who was the Best to die for we the worst.
Now if I asked you to tell me, isn't God's Love the best?
I bet your answer would be oh yes, yes, yes!
How and why does something go like this? I mean, there's nothing
free and lasts forever in this world today but God's Love, the best.
It's a shame how the people running this world
today only think about themselves and money
and not about the pain on another's chest.
But looking back at them with hate certainly
won't change their sight; besides that, as it's always
been said, two wrongs don't make a right.
It hurts so much, and it's just a shame, alright?
Like how the Pharmacies charge the Elders oh so much
for the meds they need to help ease their pain.
I mean, was it not the Elders who built this land from the very start
And has brought us oh so far mark by mark?
Yet you charge them oh so much for the Medications they need,
and this I just don't understand, but I know it's not in God's plan.
Well, I'll help them, love them, and give them hug after hug
while saying to them as if they were God, "It's you I Love."
I'm Sorry, but It Seems There's Just Nothing in This World
That's Free and Lasts Forever Anymore but God's Love!

***By** Jehovah* THROUGH THE HEART, MIND,
AND LEFT HAND OF ***Kevin Moss***

This know also, that in the last days perilous times shall come. For men shall be lovers of their own selves, covetous boasters, proud, blasphemers, disorient to parent's, unthankful, unholy.

—2 TIMOTHY 3:1–2

Forgive We All

So forgive we, forgive we, forgive we all again, again, and again.
Yes, we all must forgive all for everyone has sinned!
As it was said by my brother Paul through God our Father,
yes, when he said we all have fallen short of the glory.
And at that time, he also said there's not one good man left,
no, not one, and that's the truth and not a made-up story.
Yes, so true it truly is that everyone has made mistakes, yes,
from the top to the bottom, as well as from left to right.
But one Perfect One did walk this earth from
north to south and east to west, and I say out loud
that, that was Jesus Christ, He the Best!
But remember what He said and said it was He alone; yes, to all of
we the world, He said, "He that sinnith not cast the first stone!"
So forgive we, forgive we, forgive we all.
Yes, this we all must do, for if there's one you don't forgive
then as you won't forgive them, God won't forgive you,
So let us all forgive all with Love, Love, and more Love.
Yes, Just What Has Been Sent Down to Me, You, You, and You
Too, Coming Down from the Heavens High up Above with God's
LOVE, LOVE, AND MORE LOVE!

***By** Jehovah* THROUGH THE HEART, MIND,
AND LEFT HAND OF ***Kevin Moss***

There is no difference between the Jews and the Greek: for the same Lord over all is rich unto all that call upon Him for help.

FOR WHOSOEVER SHALL CALL UPON THE NAME OF THE LORD SHALL BE SAVED.

—ROMANS 10:12–13

Jehovah, Yes, God Is Love, Love, and More Love

Yes, *Jehovah* Is God's name who's our creator from high up above.
And believe me, He's truly nothing else but Love,
Love, and more Love, and that's all.
Yes, Love He is, and Love He's always been, and
Love He'll always be again, again, and again.
So much did He Love we the world that He
gave the life of Jesus Christ, His first and only
begotten Son, for our sins; boy, what a win!
Yes, that was surely a win, and it was a win for us all,
for once again, He died to pay for our sins.
And on top of that, it was with pure Love for us all
that He's paid the price of our sins, my friends.
HE, *JEHOVAH, EMMANUEL*, and the
HOLY GHOST, yes, GOD!
IS LOVE, LOVE, AND MORE LOVE, WITH
LOVE, LOVE, LOVE, AND MORE LOVE!

***By** Jehovah* THROUGH THE HEART, MIND,
AND LEFT HAND OF ***Kevin Moss***

A Call to Worship

O come, let us sing unto the Lord: let us make a joyful noise to the rock of our salvation. Let us come before His presence with thanksgiving, and make a joyful noise unto Him with psalms. For the Lord is a great God, and a great King above all gods. In His hands are the deep places of the earth: the strength of the hills is His also. The sea is His, and He made it: and His hands formed the dry land.

O come, let us worship and bow down: let us kneel before the Lord our maker. For He is our God; and we are the people of His pasture, and the sheep of His hand. To day if you will hear His voice, Harden not your heart, as in the provocation, and as in the day of temptation in the wilderness: When your fathers tempted me, proved me, and saw my work. Forty years long was I grieved with this generation, and said, It is a people that do err in their heart, and they have not known My ways: Unto whom I sware in my wrath that they should not enter into my rest.

—PSALM 95

Get Thy Hence

So many times and in so many ways are we tempted by the
world, yes, tempted by the world so many times we truly are.
But we're to use the world's temptation to show the
true color of our heart back to the world.
Yes, the HEART, our precious, precious pearl!
Which shows the strength, power, and faith we're
to have in He that made the heaven, earth, and
the great blue sea for all the world, yes, we!
Now inside the temple of we the world did He truly place
the heart, yes, our precious, precious pearl, you see?
I say this from my heart that it vibrates in yours so you say to that
evil one with nothing but strength you tell him from your heart!
I CAST YOU BEHIND ME, SATAN.
NOW YOU GET THY HENCE!
But please always remember and don't ever forget that today
there's so many kinds of beasts in this world inch by inch.
Yes, today there's just so many beasts in this world and they're
all after the same spark that's truly a pearl, yes, your heart.
So you must always be protected, yes, protected, and
truly are we protected by the blood of Christ.
For Jesus Christ is the best protection you could
ever have in life in the day or the night.
So with Jesus Christ by your side, just stand up to
all those ugly beasts again, again, and again.
And Just Tell Them All to Get Away from You;
yes, Tell Them to Get Thy Hence!

***By** Jehovah* THROUGH THE HEART, MIND,
AND LEFT HAND OF ***Kevin Moss***

And whosoever shall not receive you, nor hear you, when you depart thence, shake off the dust under your feet for a testimony against them. Verily I say unto you, It shall be more tolerable for Sodom and Go-mor'-rha in the day of judgment, then for that city.

—MARK 6:11

The Word Was God

"IN THE BEGINNING WAS THE WORD." The Word made
all as you heard, yes, all that was made was made by He.
He first made the heavens and then made He the earth;
just with the twinkle of an eye, He just let it burst.
Next made He the sun and the moon along with every star
you see, also every cloud in the sky, was made by He!
Yes, all these things were made by He, and believe
me, He made them all just for you and me.
Once again, He made them all just by the twinkle of an eye.
And with that same twinkle, He also made the great blue sea.
The Word made every fowl that flies in the air; He also
made all the other animals, as the great big grisly bear.
Yes, it was He that made the most and surely not the least.
It was also He that made all the mammals that swim in
the sea as well as every plant, flower, bush, and tree.
Then came the reptile, yes, the snake that moves on its belly.
And behind it came the insect.
And remember, it was all made by God's loving Grace, and with
the same Grace does He put smile after smile on face after face.
Then last but surely not least, God made man, and though
we were last in His making, we were first in His plan.
For did He not put we man, above all, yes, all that you see?
Yes, He did, and out of Love He made man, yes,
we in the image and likeness of He.
"AND THE WORD WAS WITH GOD."
And He sits at His right side; believe me, at the
right side of God He does sit, and He sits for you
and me, for it's He that makes our plea.
For He's the Father, the Son, and the Holy Ghost; yes, He
the Word was already making our plea, do not you see?
"AND THE WORD WAS GOD!"
Now after making our plea, once again out of love, He brought
Himself down from the heavens high down to the earth below.

But there's so much evil in this world we live
at times it feels like we're cursed.
He then showed us the way, promising us it would be okay
if we'd just Listen, Believe, Trust, and Follow He.
"FOR IN THE BEGINNING WAS THE WORD, and THE WORD WAS WITH GOD, and THE WORD WAS GOD!"

By** Jehovah* THROUGH THE HEART, MIND, AND LEFT HAND OF ***Kevin Moss

Jesus saith unto her, Touch me not; for I am not yet ascended to My Father: but go to my brethren, and say unto them, I ascend unto My Father, and your Father; and to My God, and your God.

—JOHN 20:17

Let Him In

He's like a breath of fresh air on a nice spring day that's been
blown out for everyone, everywhere every time we pray.
And believe me, we should all truly Love, Love,
and Love Him in every little way.
SO LET HIM IN, EVERYONE DO I SAY!
To me, it's like God the Father, through that same
breath of fresh air, also blew out of His mouth
our Lord Jesus Christ just everywhere.
SO JUST LET HIM IN; BELIEVE ME,
YOU HAVE NOTHING TO FEAR!
Now after Jesus Christ, the first Son, was blown out of the
mouth of God the Father right into the world for us all.
He, the Son, then blew out of His mouth the Comforter;
yes, He the holy Ghost will be there at our every call.
And then He the Holy Ghost blows, yes, will blow out
of His mouth for us comfort just like cotton balls.
Yes, He the Comforter will just comfort, comfort, and comfort
us with Happiness, Peace, and joy, and He'll just comfort us all.
SO YOU LET HIM IN, BIG BOY, AND YOU TOO, MY GIRL!
Yes, let Him into the heart of yours as I've let Him into mine, and
you'll feel his comfort every single day, just about all the time.
And also with comfort, the Comforter will
allow you to see his shining light; just shine, and
believe me, with love His light does just
SHINE, SHINE, SHINE!
So You Go Ahead and Just Let Him in, for Believe Me
When I Say Truly, Truly, yes, Truly It's Time!

***By** Jehovah* THROUGH THE HEART, MIND,
AND LEFT HAND OF ***Kevin Moss***

I am crucified with Christ: never the less I live; yet not I, but Christ liveth in me: and the life which I now live in the flesh I live by faith of the Son of God, who loved me, and gave Himself for me.

—GALATIANS 2:20

My Lord, My Lord, My God, Truly Do I Thank You

Oh my heavenly Father, truly do I thank You, and Jesus
Christ, my Savior, I thank You too again, again, and again.
I thank You for the air I breathe, I thank You for the food I eat,
and I thank You for all the Love You give, which truly is so sweet.
Now I know, my Lord, my Lord, my God, I
could never thank you too much.
No. I couldn't ever do that for all You've done and
given us; I just couldn't thank You enough!
So I just thank You for all Your true Love, Mercy, and Grace
that You show all and all with such a Loving touch.
Yes, My Lord, My Lord, My God, Truly Do I Thank
You for All the Love That You show us.
Yes, I thank You for all Your wonderful, wonderful
Love You send to us all from high up above.

***By** Jehovah* THROUGH THE HEART, MIND,
AND LEFT HAND OF ***Kevin Moss***

But as we were allowed of God to be put in trust with the gospel, even so we speak; not as pleasing men but God, which trieth our hearts.

—1 THESSALONIANS 2:4

For this cause also thank we God without ceasing, because, when ye received the word of God which ye heard of us, ye received it not as the word of man, but as the truth, the word of God, which effectually worketh also in you that believe.

—1 THESSALONIANS 2:13

According to the glorious gospel of the blessed God, which was committed to my trust. And thank Christ Jesus our Lord, who hath enabled me, for that He counted me faithful, putting me in the "Ministry."

—1 TIMOTHY 1:11–12

Erick, Derek, and Damon

Erick, Derek, and Damon are the names of my triplet sons,
and even though there's three to me, there's only one.
And I guess that's because when it comes to Eric, Derek,
and Damon, my love will always be the same.
And believe me, when it comes to either one
of them, my love will never change!
For yes, all three of them have really been a joy, just a joy to my heart.
Yes, believe me, they really have ever since by my lovely
wife into this world they were truly brought.
And then through nothing else but love did God give them life.
So please believe me, for they've really been just
a joy to me every single day, alright?
And it's truly just a joy watching them walk, talk, or cry,
as well as watching them play.
Now there's really not another in life but one
who even more than them do I love,
Which you should know is God, who gave them life from
high up above with His great and powerful LOVE.
Yes, God, my heavenly Father, is truly, truly just
the greatest, and this everyone should see.
And all Praise and Glory is His, and it will always be to me!
Yes, in my life, it's He that's number One, for
first He gave me such a lovely, lovely wife.
And then He gave us Erick, Derek, and Damon, our triplet
lovely sons, who too are also my friends, alright?
So I thank You, my heavenly Father, again, again, and again, and
for all the love you've shown me, I'll thank You until the very end!

***By** Jehovah* THROUGH THE HEART, MIND,
AND LEFT HAND OF ***Kevin Moss***

And He said, I will certainly return unto thee according to the time of life; and, lo, Sarah thy wife shall have a son. And Sarah heard it in the tent door, which was behind Him. Now Abraham and Sarah were old and well stricken in age; and it ceased to be with Sarah after the manner of woman. Therefore Sarah laughed within herself, saying, After I am waxed old shall I have pleasure, my lord being old also? And the Lord said unto Abraham, Wherefore did Sarah laugh, saying, Shall I of a surety bear a child, which am old? Is anything too hard for the Lord? At the time appointed I will return unto thee, according to the time of life, and Sarah will have a son.

—GENESIS 18:10–14

We Must Find a Way!

We must find a way to join as one, for God is the
Father and we're all to be in the First Son.
So we must all come together no matter what race, creed, or color.
And that's because we are one, and to the One and only
true Father are we all to be sister and brother.
Yes, we're all human beings, so we all have a head,
neck, back, and face by God's Loving Grace.
Plus, doesn't red blood run through every flesh
that's alive by that same Loving Grace?
Now to prove that we are one, we must find a way, and
yes, I do believe that we can just as well as I say.
Now with Love, Love, and more Love, let us all speed up our pace,
but believe me, LOVE is the way by that same Loving Grace.
Now may all accept this way for we're running
out of time every single day.
SO BELIEVE ME, WITH LOVE, LOVE, AND
MORE LOVE, WE MUST FIND A WAY!

***By** Jehovah* THROUGH THE HEART, MIND,
AND LEFT HAND OF ***Kevin Moss***

And He said unto him, Why callest thou Me good? There is none good but One, that is, God: but if thou wilt enter into life, keep the commandments. He saith unto Him, Which? Jesus said, THOUGH SHALT DO NO MURDER, THOU SHALT NOT COMMIT ADULTERY, THOU SHALT NOT STEAL, THOU SHALT NOT BEAR FALSE WITNESS, HONOUR THY FATHER AND THY MOTHER: and THOU SHALT LOVE THY NEIGHBOUR AS THY SELF.

—MATTHEW 19:17–19

Grace, Grace, Grace

God, who created the Heavens, the Earth, as well as the Sea,
created it all with such a loving grace for every one of we.
Yes, He gracefully created it with the same magnificent
grace that He created both you and me.
Grace is showing lovingkindness to all, as is opening a door for a
Lady, just like it is if one helps up another if they happened to fall.
Yes, that's Grace, Grace, Grace, Amazing Grace, you-al!
Saying your grace, thanking God for the food
you're about to eat truly, truly pleases Him, as does
saying "thank you" and "please" to others.
Yes, it pleases Him oh so much that He cleans for you whatever
you're about to eat, with Grace, Grace, Grace, and more Grace.
Grace is also one we should show to all, all,
and all, so please upper your pace!
Kindness is grace; yes, it's as great as helping another when they're
hurt; grace is just being there for them whenever they call.
So as God has always Gracefully been here for
us, may we graciously, greatly, and gratefully be
there also to help each other wall to wall?
Yes, let us all be there for all, all, and all with
grace, yes, both you and me, you-al!
WHICH IS GRACE, GRACE, GRACE FOR
LOVE IS AMAZING, AMAZING; YES, IT'S
JUST AMAZING GRACE, YAWL!

***By** Jehovah* THROUGH THE HEART, MIND,
AND LEFT HAND OF ***Kevin Moss***

He answered and said unto them, Because it is given unto you to know the mysteries of the Kingdom of heaven, but to them it is not given. For whosoever hath, to him shall be given, and he shall have more abundance; but whosoever hath not, from him shall be taken away even that he hath.

—MATTHEW 13:11–12

Love, Peace, and Soul with Happiness, Peace, and Joy

Love with peace truly eases the soul!
Yes, as happiness with peace brings one so much joy without
hurt and pain, but just with joy, joy, joy and more joy.
So let's respect one another for that will give
happiness, peace, and joy to all girls and boys.
Love is God, and peace you get from He with no worry in the soul,
for the soul is God, who's in both me and you in whole, true?
Happiness with Love, Love, and more Love brings
peace and joy and togetherness too!
Respect are we to show each other every day for then
are we really showing God's Love and Way.
Yes, we are to be as God the Father, God the Son, and
God the Holy Ghost for like He from high above,
we're to also be Love, Love, and more Love.
And remember from the three one from high
up above are we first shown Love.
LOVE, WITH LOVE, PEACE, and SOUL
COMING WITH HAPPINESS, PEACE, and JOY
IS TRULY GOD, WHO'S LOVE, TRUE?
YES, IT IS, BUT ALWAYS REMEMBER and NEVER FORGET
THAT LOVE IS LOVE, and more LOVE IS ALSO GOD TOO.

***By** Jehovah* THROUGH THE HEART, MIND,
AND LEFT HAND OF ***Kevin Moss***

Even so ye also outwardly appear righteous unto men, but within ye are full of hypocrisy and iniquity.

—MATTHEW 23:28

And why call Me Lord, Lord and do not the things which I say?

—LUKE 6:46

My little children let us not love in word, neither in tongue; but in deed and in truth.

—1 JOHN 3:18

H20

Another thing we ought to thank God for I'd say is "H_2O."
Remember, it was from the dew of His heavens that
He made the Great Blue Sea just for we.
And it was through that great blue sea that
He saved the Jews, didn't He?
Yes, God had them march and follow Moses from one side to the other.
And as God told the Jews to follow Moses through,
Pharaoh also told the Egyptians to follow them too.
But with God's H_2O, which at the time was
just called the great blue sea.
God first split it in half and then dropped it on Pharaoh's whole army.
Plus, in the great blue sea that God made for we swims all the
fish that are good for the brain and also so sweet to eat.
Then from the rain falling from the sky to the earth, again His H_2O!
Truly does it feed all the beautiful plants that God also made.
Yes, it's through God's sun and His H_2O that they truly do grow!
And always remember and never forget that all those wonderful
plants grow here on earth right with me and you.
So we really do owe God so much thanks with a lot of glory and praise.
Now let us come together as one to thank He the
Lord, for aren't we all to be in His Son?
Yes, we are, so we must, we must, we must
all thank Him for all His show.
AND LET US NEVER FORGET THAT
TOO INCLUDES HIS H_2O!

***By** Jehovah* THROUGH THE HEART, MIND,
AND LEFT HAND OF ***Kevin Moss***

And the Lord said unto Moses, "Stretch out thine hand over the sea, that the waters may come again upon the Egyptians, upon their chariots and upon their horsemen." And Moses stretched forth his hand over the sea, and the sea returned to his strength when the morning appeared; and the Egyptians fled against it; and the Lord overthrew the Egyptians in the midst of the sea.

—EXODUS 14:26–28

You Can Have More Than One

There's a lot of sayings you've heard and you'll come to see are true.
But some you'll also come to see aren't too.
No, for a lot of those old sayings you've heard
are nothing but words from the past.
And a lot of their meanings weren't true or just didn't last.
For instance, take this one, which is one that so many
times I heard my mother use and say, yes, so many
times she'd say, "YOU ONLY GET ONE!"
And for so many years, I believed it, but I've
just come to see that it really isn't true.
Believe me, it isn't, no, it really isn't true,
for you can have more than one.
Now the reason I know this is because God, my
Heavenly Father, with His Loving Grace, has just sent
me my wife putting a great big smile on my face.
Believe me, for from the bottom of my heart, I do tell you the truth.
It seems God has just sent my wife from the heavens
straight down to me from high up above.
And from God's Loving Grace, her mom is still with us today.
But unfortunately, mine, who I loved so very
much, has already passed away.
Now the point here that I'm trying to make is plainly said as so.
Mom, I already know you're good, and I also
know You truly do believe, true?
And on top of that, I also know she gets all hers from you!
So I ask you, Mom, do you also believe me when
I say that God has already told me?
Yes, He told me that truly, truly, truly she's the one!
And that once again through His Loving Grace, I
have another mother and you have another son,
Which should make it clear to all for it's
nothing but the truth, everyone.
Yes, it is so true going out to a mother coming from a son.

Proving to all, all, and all without a single doubt, everyone.
IT'S so, so TRUE THAT YOU CAN HAVE MORE THAN ONE!

***By** Jehovah* THROUGH THE HEART, MIND,
AND LEFT HAND OF ***Kevin Moss***

For He saith to Moses, I WILL HAVE MERCY ON WHOM I WILL HAVE MERCY, AND I WILL HAVE COMPASSION ON WHOM I WILL HAVE COMPASSION. So then it is not of him that willeth, nor of him that runneth, but of God. that sheweth mercy.

—ROMANS 9:15–16

One Wonderful Two That Are Truly Only One

Here We Have Two That Have the Same Love for All.
Yes, They Do, for They'll Both Be There for
You As One Whenever You May Call.
Believe Me, They'll Be There to Pick You
Up If You Ever Happen to Fall.
For Their Two That Would Pick Anyone Up, For
They Have the Same Sweet, Sweet Love for All.
YES, THEIR ONE WONDERFUL TWO
THAT ARE TRULY ONLY ONE!
Believe Me, They Know, Believe, and Hold in
Their Heart That We're All Only One.
Jehovah Being the Father and We Being the Son,
Such a Lovely Two That Are Only One.
YES, SO TRUE THEY TRULY ARE ONE WONDERFUL
TWO THAT ARE TRULY ONLY ONE.

***By** Jehovah* THROUGH THE HEART, MIND,
AND LEFT HAND OF ***Kevin Moss***

But be not ye called Rabbi: for one is your Master, even Christ; and all ye are brethren. And call no man your father upon the earth: for one is your Father, which is in heaven. Neither be ye called masters: for one is your Master, even Christ.

—MATTHEW 23:8–10

God's Good

God's good, good. He is good, He's always been
good and He'll always be my friends.
God's so good that He first created man, and with love,
He then gave him life, again, again, and again.
Plus, even after wrong was done by the first human being, and
life we lost; God's just so good that He gave it back to us again.
YES, GOD'S SO GOOD THAT HE SENT HIS FIRST
SON DOWN FROM HEAVEN TO PAY THE COST.
Yes, God's so good and nice that He allowed Jesus
Christ, His only begotten Son, to die for us and give
us back eternal life, which we had surely lost.
That's right, His first Son came down from heaven
to His earth, where He was nailed to a cross and
died for us; odd, but still it was a plus.
To us, that shouldn't be odd, and believe me, it was for He's so
good, and His name is Jesus Christ, who's another form of God.
NOW DO YOU SEE, SEE, SEE THE REAL LIGHT?

By *Jehovah* THROUGH THE HEART, MIND,
AND LEFT HAND OF ***Kevin Moss***

The Lord of hosts is with us; the God of Jacob is our refuge. Selah. Come, behold the works of the Lord, what desolations He hath made in the earth. He maketh wars to Cease unto the end of the earth; he breaketh the bow, and cutteth the spear in sunder; He burneth the chariot in the fire. Be still, and know that I am God: I will be exalted in the earth. The Lord of hosts is with us; the God of Jacob is our refuge. Selah.

—PSALM 46:7–11

Turn the Other Cheek

Sometimes one can make another oh so mad, and
that other just wants to get even oh so bad.
Now I know how one can feel after being let down by another!
But still it's good for us to always remember what Mother
always said; you remember what she'd always say.
That's right, she'd say, "*Two Wrongs Doesn't Make a Right, Okay*?"
Let us also not forget that the other is your sister or brother,
which applies to us all for we all come together.
Yes, we all do come together, no matter what race, creed, or color.
So Turn the Other, Turn the Other, Yes, Turn the Other Cheek!
Yes, just let our Lord Jesus Christ change your heart,
mind, and body's whole rhythm and beat.
Now we find in the book of Exodus 21:24—eye for eye
and tooth for tooth, hand for hand, and foot for foot.
And that was fair once upon a time; in fact, it was the way, but
again, it was once upon another time, which was just yesterday.
Which was also before we were filled with the Holy Ghost.
Yes, filled by the Love, Blood, Power, and Grace of our
Lord Jesus Christ, I must say, so let us do it His way!
By Turning the Other Cheek, Turning the Other Cheek,
Yes, Everyone, Please Turn the Other Cheek.
Plus, along with our hearts and minds, may we also let He, the
Lord of Lords and King of Kings, change the movement in our feet.
Just Turn the Other, Turn the Other, Turn the Other Cheek, and
Follow the Steps of Jesus Christ No Matter How Steep or Deep,
Which means if one takes away your cloak, also give him your
coat; if another asks you to run a mile, tell him you'll run two.
Believe me, God will give you all the strength you need.
He'll also take away your blue, and turning
the other Cheek is all you have to do.

***By** Jehovah* THROUGH THE HEART, MIND,
AND LEFT HAND OF ***Kevin Moss***

For even hereunto were ye called: because Christ also suffered for us, leaving us an example, that ye should follow His steps: WHO DID NO SIN, NEITHER WAS GUILE FOUND IN HIS MOUTH: Who when He was reviled, reviled not again; when He suffered, He threatened not; but committed Himself to Him that judgeth righteously.

—1 PETER 2:21–23

The Bright Shining Light

You know, our world has so many different types of shining lights.
The funny thing is that the brightest of them
are, half of the time, out of sight.
Take the star; yes, the star a light that's oh so bright is the star.
They're so bright that you can see them just about wherever you are.
Yes, the star has such a bright, bright shine that
we're wishing on them all the time.
Many times we're wishing on a star for such a
bright shining light they truly, truly are.
How about the moon? Another bright shining
light that truly, truly shines in the night.
And it's just so beautiful too as it shine its light down on me and you.
And even though it shines in the night, it's still so beautiful to see.
Yes, as they shine their lights down on both you and me.
Yes, the star does shine so bright, and it's so
lovely to see them shine in the night.
And all the different shapes and sizes the moon
makes has always fascinated my sight.
But next to the brightest light of all is surely the sun.
But it's the other Son that's number one!
Still through the power of the bright shining sun, all does grow for we.
Yes, every plant, flower, bush, and tree does grow
for us all, yes, for both you and me.
But let's not forget about every string of green, green grass that we see.
Still as before, the brightest light of all is the
first Son of God, and that's for sure!
Yes, it's He that's the Bright Shining Light!
And it's also He you call in your times of need, whether day or night.
Yes, Jesus Christ is the One to call, for He gave
His life paying the wage of sin for us all.
I think you got it, yes, that it's Jesus Christ that's
THE BRIGHT SHINING LIGHT!

By** Jehovah* THROUGH THE HEART, MIND, AND LEFT HAND OF ***Kevin Moss

For with the heart man believeth unto righteousness; and with the mouth confession is made unto salvation.

—ROMANS 10:10

For there is no difference between the Jew and the Greek: for the same Lord over all is rich unto all that call upon Him.

FOR WHOSOEVER SHALL CALL UPON THE NAME OF THE LORD SHALL BE SAVED.

—ROMANS 10:12–13

There's Only One I Praise and Bow Down To!

There's only 1 I praise and bow down to, and
if you're not God, it surely isn't you!
For only God do I give all my praise and glory to!
I mean, should I not since it's truly His anyway?
For He made the Heavens, the Earth, and
the Great Blue Sea, didn't He?
On top of that, he even made the air we breathe, do not you see?
Yes, God made everything of life, what you don't see, and what you do!
Yes, that's right, if it has life, it was first made
and given life by He, alright?
So there's only 1 I praise and bow down to every day and night!
Remember, it was God who made both the Sun
and the Moon, yes, He's the True Light!
And don't forget, God also made every star you see that are oh so bright.
And God has so much power that He placed
everyone where He wanted it to be, alright.
So God's the One I give all my praise and glory to.
But the question I now ask is, what about you?
But think about it, and then ask yourself, out
of all that He's done for me and you,
Shouldn't He be the only One We praise and bow down to?
Yes, I really think He should, yes, I do, I do,
I do, and you should too, TRUE?

***By** Jehovah* THROUGH THE HEART, MIND,
AND LEFT HAND OF ***Kevin Moss***

And God spake all these words, saying, I am the Lord thy God that brought thee out of the land of EGYPT, out of the house of bondage. Thou shalt have no other gods before Me. Thou shalt not make unto thee any graven image, or any likeness of anything that is in heaven above, or the earth beneath, or that is in the water under the earth: Thou shah not bow down thyself to them, nor serve them: for I the Lord thy God am a jealous God, visiting the iniquity of the fathers upon the children unto the third and fourth generation of them that hate Me; And shewing mercy unto thousands of them that love Me and keep My commandments.

—EXODUS 20:1–5

First Is Last and Top Is Bottom

There's just so many today that put themselves
first and think that they're on top.
But believe me, by the Word of God, their last
and will be on the bottom, not the top!
There's still a lot of people in the world today that may be on the top.
But the top that they're on is the currency
that's really not top; it's bottom!
For in the end, followed by the new beginning,
it will put them on the bottom.
For What Was Said by God Was, He on the Top Shall Be on the Bottom
And He That's First Will Be Last!
And to them, I say, don't forget about the words
of the first rich man who was cast down.
You remember what he said, don't you?
Well, if you don't, his words were said in the
book of Luke 16:24, and he cried.
"Father Abraham, have mercy on me, and send Lazarus
that he may dip his finger in some water to cool my
tongue, for I am tormented in this flame."
So to you, my brothers and sisters of the
poor, do I say, where's your faith?
DON'T YOU BELIEVE GOD?
Remember it was He who clearly said:
"He That Is First Will Be Last and He on
the Top Will Be on the Bottom!"
Now if you just hold that in your heart, you'll
see it will fill your every pocket.
And on top of that, it will also put true power in your every socket!
Now let a big Amen from us shoot up to God just like a rocket.
AMEN, AMEN, AMEN!

***By** Jehovah* THROUGH THE HEART, MIND,
AND LEFT HAND OF ***Kevin Moss***

And He lifted up His eyes on His disciples, and said, Blessed be ye poor: for your's is the kingdom of God. Blessed are ye that hunger now: for ye shall be filled. Blessed are ye that weep now: for you shall laugh.

—LUKE 6:20

But woe unto you that are rich! For ye have received your consolation.

—LUKE 6:24

Chaos or Love, Who's Your Choice?

It seems in the world today we see almost
nothing but chaos day after day.
Yes, so much chaos we see today as if we're living in nothing
but a chaotic mixed-up world, would not you say?
It seems people today have nothing on their minds but
how to hurt one while bringing down another.
Yes, just like their chaotic filled with nothing but chaos, and just
as we see them, so does our heavenly Father also see them.
But, all my sisters and brothers, to follow God and
to rightly Love is just another way to be.
And since God is Love, to Love is also the right way to be, you see?
So don't ever let chaos roam in your heart or float in your mind.
No, instead, let God's Love fill you up, and it'll
force chaos out of your life every single time.
Now Love is just showing respect with kindness to all,
and chaos is preparing yourself for a big downfall.
Yes, through chaos down, down you'll go into a big fire, and
there you'll eternally burn forever, ever and ever, you know?
But Love will clean you up and set you free, for
Love is God do I say once again by words coming
out of my mouth to you all, you see?
And coming out of the same mouth at a different tone of
voice do I also ask you, Chaos or Love? Who's your choice?

***By** Jehovah* THROUGH THE HEART, MIND,
AND LEFT HAND OF ***Kevin Moss***

But chiefly them that walk after the flesh in the lust of uncleanness, and despise government. Presumptuous are they, self-willed, they are not afraid to speak evil of dignities. Whereas angels, which are greater in power and might, bring not railing accusation against them before the Lord. But these, as natural brute beasts, made to be taken and destroyed, speak evil of things that they understand not; and shall utterly perish in their own corruption; And shall receive the reward of unrighteousness, as they that count it pleasure to riot in the day time. Spots they are and blemishes, sporting themselves with their own deceiving's while they feast with you.

—2 PETER 2:10–13

You Can't Escape the Eclipse

You can't, you can't, you just can't escape the eclipse.
I mean, do you really think you can escape God's judgment?
Yes, here the word *eclipse* means judgment, the day
we'll all reap what we sowed, you know?
And believe me, it's one step in life that we
all will have to take one day, and go.
For it's that one time that Jesus said that all would bow to
He, and that He would judge every single one of we.
NO, YOU CAN'T ESCAPE THE ECLIPSE; NO,
WE CAN'T, WHICH MEANS YOU, ME, HE,
SHE, NOR ANYONE ELSE, YOU SEE?
But You know what's funny, today a lot of human
beings are still creating all kinds of Rockets and
Spaceships just trying to find a way.
Yes, they're still trying to find a way to live in
space, which is something that will never ever take
place no matter what color, creed, or race.
It's God that created us as He first created the heavens, the earth,
and the sea, and this is where He placed us and wanted us to be.
Yes, here on earth is where He placed all of we to be until He
comes back to get both you and me and all that belongs to He.
And as He said, when He comes back, we all will bow down
to He, and then He'll judge every single one of we,
SO YOU CAN'T ESCAPE THE ECLIPSE.
WHY THIS CAN'T MAN BELIEVE OR SEE,
WILL SOMEONE PLEASE TELL ME?

***By** Jehovah* THROUGH THE HEART, MIND,
AND LEFT HAND OF ***Kevin Moss***

> Knowing this first, that there shall come in the last days scoffers, walking after their own lusts, And saying, Where is the promise of his coming? For since the fathers fell asleep, all things continue as they were from the beginning of the creation. For this they willingly are ignorant of, that by the word of God the heavens were of old, and the earth standing out of the water and in the water: Where the world that then was, being overflowed with water perished: But the heavens and the earth, which are now by the same word are kept in store, reserved unto fire against the day of judgment and perdition of ungodly men. But beloved, be not ignorant of this one thing, that one day is with the Lord as a thousand years, and a thousand years as one day.
>
> —2 Peter 3:3–8

> For if God spared not the angels that sinned, but cast them down to hell, and delivered them into chains of darkness, to be reserved for judgement; And spared not the old world, but saved Noah the eighth person, a preacher of righteousness, bringing in the flood upon the world of the ungodly.
>
> —2 PETER 2:4–5

DO YOU REALLY THINK YOU SHALL ESCAPE HE?

Love and Need Are Two Different Things

Love and Need are two different things, just two.
Yes, they're two very different things; now
you understand this, don't you?
Now Love, we're to Love, but money, we're not.
For we were created by Love, with Love, for Love is our Maker.
But the US currency is nothing but paper, and
if we must, we can go without paper.
But we just can't go without Love, again the One who's truly our Maker!
Now while we're still in the flesh living on
earth, we need money to survive,
for it's what we use to feed and clothe ourselves in life.
But we're to first Love God, for God Is and also gave us Life, right?
BUT LOVE AND NEED ARE STILL TWO
DIFFERENT THINGS, ALRIGHT?
Now there are so many different things that we all surely do need,
But we also have One that truly Loves and also needs us all,
AND THAT'S GOD, OUR HEAVENLY FATHER, YOU-AL.
BELIEVE ME, LOVE AND NEED ARE
TRULY TWO DIFFERENT THINGS!
Yes, they truly are two different things, you know what I mean?

***By** Jehovah* THROUGH THE HEART, MIND,
AND LEFT HAND OF ***Kevin Moss***

Finally, be ye all of one mind, having compassion one of another, love as brethren, be pitiful, be courteous: Not rendering evil for evil, or railing for railing: but contrariwise blessing; knowing that ye are thereunto called, that ye should inherit a blessing FOR HE THAT WILL LOVE LIFE, AND SEE GOOD DAYS, LET HIM REFRAIN HIS TONGUE FROM EVIL, AND HIS LIPS THAT THEY SPEAK NO GUILE.

—1 PETER 3:8–10

Let God Put Us Back Together

You know today it seems a lot of our lives are just so messed
up that at times we seem like a great big puzzle.
And on top of that, it seems most of the world wants
to treat us like asses wearing real tight muzzles.
Believe me, Satan wants to keep us all mixed up
that at times we feel like those five hundred pieces
that end up making a beautiful picture.
Yes, just like we, it too started out as nothing
but a mixed-up puzzle for sure.
BUT LET'S, LET GOD PUT US BACK TOGETHER, AND
BELIEVE ME, WORLD, HE'LL MEET US AT THE DOOR.
It just seems like so many of we the world are just so
unfair today, and why's that, would you say?
I mean, God made it so clear that we come with
nothing and we'll leave with nothing,
so why do so many of us so badly hurt ourselves
by first hurting others? I just don't know.
But what I do know is that we all do come together, so
we all should Love, Love, and more Love each other.
Yes, we should, no matter what race, creed, or color, for that doesn't
matter at all because still you're my sister or you're my brother.
Believe me, we're just one big family, so let's just let God, who
made us also put us back together, all my sisters and brothers.

By *Jehovah* THROUGH THE HEART, MIND,
AND LEFT HAND OF ***Kevin Moss***

Father let us be one against the glory I had
with you before this world was created.
—JOHN 17:5

Charge them that are rich in this world, that they be not highminded, nor trust in uncertain riches, but in the living God, who giveth us richly all things to enjoy; That they do good, that they be rich in works ready to distribute, willing to communicate; Laying up in store for themselves a good foundation against the time to come, that they may lay hold of eternal life.

—1 TIMOTHY 6:17–19

He's Been A Cloud Over Me All My Life Part 2

NOW FOR A MOMENT MAY I BE A CLOUD OVER YOURS?

Now I'm sure you've read all of the poems in love, love, and more love for every one of them are just so beautiful, unique, and true for Jehovah; yes, God is the true author of every one of them, and He's worked through my heart and mind by inspiration bringing it out of my left hand just for all of you, and I just know you couldn't stop reading them until you were through, true? Now all my life, He's been a cloud over me, and I now ask you if, by His love, may He use me at the moment to be a cloud over yours? Believe me, I just want to try to break down some things for you, just some of what we're going through today, hoping I may draw a spark in some of your hearts, helping you to understand, as God, through the Lord Jesus Christ and the Holy Ghost, first helped me. And believe me, He did tell me just like He also told you to be fruitful and multiply, so let's go here with the truth and take off on a natural high. Now I ask you, all the world, still don't you realize and believe that there's only one God and that this earth we now live on is first His and that everything on it with life is also His? Yes, from the stars in the sky down to the green grass below, you know? Which also very clearly tells us that we need Him, He doesn't need us, which in its own way was, is, and will always be a *great big plus*, for all He's shown from His first making of man has been nothing but love, love, and more love, and once again, He's shown it to us all. We all just don't take it and believe it. For again, it was He who created all things of life, which we so surely need, yes, from the air we breathe to the food we eat. Yes, it was God that made for us every herb-bearing seed which are in a lot of the foods we eat, yes, every bush, flower, and tree, and this do not you see? But then after all His making, the first two and only human beings He made with His bare hands sinned and brought death upon us all. But God was still so full of love that He came back with love, love, and more love by sending His first and only begotten Son from the heavens high down to His earth below just to die and give us another chance to live, but why? Now someone try and tell me that, that's not a Father, a true brother, and a best, best friend in one, and I'll then tell them that they're liars again, again, and again! But the real problem is that it seems that so many of we the world still don't understand that we all the world do truly need very, very much that true, true brother and best, best friend to be accepted by God, who's our true, true Father and the very first man, and we were all made in His image and likeness, which, from the very start, was part of His plan. But the main thing I don't understand, don't believe, and just don't get is that today we still have so many people that are still judging others by the color of their skin or by the language that they speak when not one of us should be judging anyone, and that goes for both me and you, true? Remember, this is God's earth, and when He gave us all life, He also gave us the right to walk His earth, am not I right? Believe me, God has no favorites for truly He loves us all. Tell me, do you believe that coronavirus has a favorite. I mean, is it not taking life from every country, state, city, and town, as well as just about every family out here today that's truly still around? Yes, it's taking life from so many families no matter what race, creed, or color they are from every country, state, city, and town. And when it comes to saying things like "It was made in China," really doesn't make any sense. And what kind of a person is one that believes the economy is more important than the people? I mean, the economy is the salesman and the buyer, right? But if by coronavirus, all your salesmen and buyers are dead, you then have no economy, do you? So how can the economy be more important than the people? That also doesn't make any sense, if you ask me, does it? Believe me, still today just like yesterday,

God is still the only one that can give and take life inch by inch. But dig this and tell me, what do you get from it? We find in the Holy Bible in the book of Micah 6:12–13 "Your rich men are violent. They exploit the poor. Their tongues are deceitful, and they lie without hesitation. There for I will destroy your land because of your sins, I've begun to smite you by letting you become sick." Hell of a thought, don't you think? I know I do! Yes, it is, and don't forget about this, yes, please remember, you-al, for if I'm not mistaken this He did say, and He also said it more than once: "*My Word shall always stand!*" And believe me, they will! So who do we listen to? God or the United States government? Now I try not to judge, but as everyone else, I do sometimes too, but I try my best to as God said to, go off the heart and mind. Now the heart pretty much tells you what kind of person that person is, and the mind tells you of a person's intelligence. Now I don't know about you, but I try my best to listen and follow God to the best of my ability, and believe me, it's all in His Word for He didn't leave anything out. Now God the Son once said, "The love of money is the root of all evil!" Now as I just said, I listen to God now and go off the heart and the mind, and once again God's Word tells us everything. Now if you ask me, all our Ex-President Donald Trump seemed to think about and, most of the time, talk about was money, so it really looks like he loves it, to me, and if he does, it also shows that he's evil, for remember, that's what God said, isn't it? Yes, the love of money is the root of all evil! I also ask you again, who do we believe, God or Donald Trump? Now we know for a fact that God doesn't lie; remember, God's the one that made one of His laws, "Thou shall not bear false witness unto thy neighbor," right? But I've also watched and listened to Donald Trump lie right in my face on national television, so don't try and tell me he doesn't lie! So how can I follow someone like him, when God also said, "If the blind lead the blind, they both shall fall in the ditch." And it sure looks like he's going down, if you ask me. Now let me share something else with you on God, Donald Trump, and myself, and everything I say is the truth. The year, 2020, will be the first year I have ever voted in my life, for I just never had any entrance in politics before Donald Trump. Now he ran for a senate seat three other times and lost and in 2016 when he was running against Mrs. Hillary Clinton for President I used to look at a lot of the debates between them. Now the first thing that always turned me off about Donald Trump was, it seemed at every one of the debates between him and Ms. Clinton, every time they would ask Donald Trump a question, he would always first try to push the question on Mrs. Clinton, until they would finally say, "We didn't ask her the question, we asked you," and no matter what the question was, the answer he came back with would always be something about money. Now after one of their debates, I tried to turn the television knob to change the station for the debate was over, but for some reason, the knob wouldn't turn, so I just sat back down on the bed and kept looking at the TV, trying to figure out what was wrong, and the next thing I know, something was coming on where a reporter was going to interview Donald Trump after the debate between him and Ms. Clinton. Now this might sound crazy, but believe me, it's true. When the show came on with the reporter interviewing Donald Trump, it really took me out, for even though I had just looked at him in the debate, still when I first saw him come on to the screen of the TV, I didn't see Donald Trump as a human being; I saw a devil. As I looked at it, I said out loud, "Oh my god, that's a devil!" Now I know it had to be God to allow me to see what I saw, for who else could make me see it but God? And besides that, when I looked at the reporter, I didn't see a devil; I saw a Caucasian male, so why didn't I see that when I looked at Donald Trump? I also believed the word *devil* meant "Satan," but at the very time when I saw what I saw, the Holy Spirit made me go into the dictionary and look up the word *devil*, and I came to find out at the time that the word *devil* meant "an evil, evil person"! And believe me, this all took me out so much that I even went on Facebook and wrote that I just saw Donald Trump as a devil. And you know, something else that really took me out was, I looked at the whole thing from beginning to end, and not one question that the reporter asked Donald Trump did he directly answer besides the last question, which was when the reporter asked him, how did he get out of not paying the tax money he owed when he sold Trump Towers? Donald Trump then got out of his seat, stuck his chest out, and said, "Oh, I'm good at that," which I took to mean he was good at cheating, for he sure is. For really, he's torn this country apart since he's been in office, and there's been nothing in the White House since he's been there but chaos, if you ask me, so believe me, everyone; we all better start listening to God while we still can, and believe me, we're truly running out of time. So instead of us continuing going up against each other, trying to make oneself look better than the other, let us human beings with love start coming together with love, love, and more love forever, ever and ever, for as both the Father and the Son, we too are also one, one, one.

Now in the month of May in the year of 2020, the USA once again plans to send a few astronauts back into space, but my question is, why? For believe me, man is never going to find a way to live in space. Again, believe me, God put us here on His earth, and on His earth is where we shall remain until Jesus Christ, His first Son and our Lord and Savior, comes back to earth once again from heaven to get all that's His. If God meant for man to be in space, He would have put a few of us up there, don't you think? Anyway, until He comes back to get us, on this earth is where we shall remain, yes, right here on this earth. How about looking at it like this for a moment and let's see then what you think? First of all, remember, the Holy Bible was originally written by God Himself. Yes, He used fifty-two different men to put it on paper; in other words, He inspired them of what to write then just as He's now inspiring me what to write now, but believe me, God is still the author. Now I know over the years, Satan has also used a lot of people to take out as well as put in a lot of different things in the Bible because he doesn't want us to know the truth. But most of the Bible is still the same; believe me, it is. Now in a few months, I'll be sixty years old, and as I said earlier, I've been reading this book over, over, and over since I was seventeen; again, I tell you the truth. Now I remember reading a part of the Bible back then and still read the same thing now, and this is a part that I think plainly tells us that we'll never live in space. Now here I must start again with God as the true author of the Bible, and all the times Jesus Christ spoke in the Bible, it was truly God the Father talking through Him. Now there's a part in the Bible where Jesus Christ truly said, "All shall bow to me and I shall judge all!" Now first of all, He did say all, didn't He? And believe me, when He said it, He truly meant every one of you and me; in fact, everyone that has ever walked this earth will first bow to He, God the Son, and then will be judged by He, God the Son, besides two, and those two are Adam and Eve for they've already been judged, and since death is the wage of sin, believe me, they'll never live again. But through God's love and His Son, He gave you and me another chance to win. But please believe me, once again, not one person shall ever live in space, and we all shall bow to Jesus Christ before we are judged by Him, and we know this will happen, and you see, if one person doesn't bow to God the Son or if God the Son doesn't judge one person, that would make God the Father a liar; since God the Father is the true author, it was He that said, "All shall bow to me and I shall judge all," and God doesn't lie, so there's no way one can be in space, for we'll all be there at the time of judgment. Now Jesus Christ said those resting in peace shall be the first to meet Him in the sky and all the ones still walking the earth will follow behind. Now do you understand why we'll never be able to live in space? And what do you think now? Believe me, there's only one Savior, Jesus Christ! And since we won't be able to ever live in space, for man to blow so much money up in smoke over, over, and over again, again, and again time after time is really stupid, if you ask me, for it's truly wasting a whole lot of money and also a whole lot of time when there are so many other things it can be used for that are so much more important than trying to do something that's never going to be done. Now maybe if we stop having so much hate for each other but as God informed us to do, that we learn to love, respect, and accept each other for who they are no matter what race, creed, or color, we may come to be and learn to be sisters and brothers living in happiness, peace, and joy. Now again do I say that God is the Genius of geniuses for He gave man the intelligence to invent things like the car, train and air plane, as well as all the other positive inventions man came up with today. For, yes, God has given us all a gift of some kind, for it was He who gave us the heart, brain, and mind. Now once again, I also ask you to remember what Jesus once said with so much heart. I ask you to always remember it with just as much heart, for once again, that was really God talking to us all when He said, "All shall bow to me, and

I shall judge all!" And from the ways of the world today, that doesn't seem too far away, if I may say, and really I must say we're getting closer and closer to that time every single day. So it's really time that we all the world try real love again, yes, real love, only this time we must use it a new way and the right way, as God first did say. Now the right way is to accept your brother however he may come, and it's to do it as said by God the Father, yes, with love, love and more love: "Accept your brother however he may come, my son." Now once in the book of Acts 4:19, Peter and John replied, whether it was more important to listen to God or man, something that had to be decided between them, and now I ask you the same question, for instance in 2016, I saw and heard our President Donald Trump on TV at an NFL game say that we're supposed to praise the American flag and that anyone that didn't shouldn't be allowed to work in the United States. But we find written in the book of Exodus 20:35 "Thou shalt have no other gods before Me. Thou shalt not make any graven image, or any likeness of anything that is in heaven above, the earth beneath or the water under the earth. Thou shalt not bow down thyself to them, nor serve them for I the Lord thy God am a jealous God." Now these are true words of God; in fact, these words are part of His Ten Commandments, yes, God's true law and will. So as both my brothers Peter and John asked whether it was more important to listen to God or man; as I also said before, world, I now ask you the same question, again, again, and again. But Peter and John answered and said unto themselves, "Whether it be right in the sight of God to hearken unto you more than unto God, judge ye" (Acts 4:19). Now I also remember seeing that day while looking at the game a player of the San Francisco 49ers being fired from his job, because when asked to stand up and praise the American flag, he went down to his knees, and I'm sure by him doing that, it's God that he impressed, for only God are we to praise, whether we're standing on our feet or kneeling on our knees. But you know, another thing that seems so hard to get so many other human beings to understand and believe is that you can't be saved by money! And the main reason for that is that you can't buy God; no, you can't, for God's just not for sale, and at the end as well as the new beginning, there are only two destinations for man to land,

and that's heaven or hell! And to avoid ending up in the worst destination there is or could ever be, which is hell if you ask me, there's only one Savior, and that's God's first Son, Jesus Christ, the saving Messiah who's truly number one! But it seems today so many people take this as some kind of joke, fairy tale, or just a made-up story, but when we get to the stage of judgment, believe me, there are so many that won't be laughing anymore; no, they'll be crying. Once again, believe me, for I'm really not playing when I say this, nor am I joking when I say it, nor am I joking when I say that we the world are truly running out of time, for when Christ comes back through those clouds, all of us that are not washed clean by His blood when the trumpet is blown by the angels on both His sides all sinners shall definitely be cast down, yes, just like toast in a fire, you know? Which is a fire that won't ever be going out, and believe me, who's ever cast in it won't ever be getting out, but as my Father surely did say, "They shall eternally burn!"

Now I understand how the family of George Floyd must have felt after losing a son, brother, and friend all at once, and plus, losing him in the way that they lost him must have made it hurt even more, and you can best believe just about everyone feels the same way when, by God, one's number is called, whether it's the number of a family member or just a friend, for I'm sure that person's family members and friends loved them just that much. But believe, my *world*, yes, I say to you, all my sisters and brothers, we must all face the fact that one day all our numbers will be called, for death is just another part of life, and that's because it's something we shall all experience one day. Now the officer that knelt on Mr. Floyd's neck until he brought death unto his flesh was wrong, for another one of God's laws so truly is, "Thou shall not kill!" But please also believe that it really wasn't the officer that really took Mr. Floyd's life; it was God, for there's no one that can give or take life but God, He who first gave it, and that's because life is truly His! Now once again, I ask you to believe me when I say that Mr. Floyd and anyone else that has already been called from this life before the next arrival of our Lord, Jesus Christ, are not really dead; no, they're now resting in peace, and remember, Jesus Christ did say that they would be the first to meet Him in the sky, and believe me, they will! But the world today is just filled with so much evil, I must say. And we the world aren't helping it get any better today.

For instance, I believe TV is one of the biggest problems we have today, for all you see on it any more is nothing but shows with a lot of murdering, robbing, and raping, yes, just a whole lot of wrong. What happened to television? I mean, when all the world today sees on it is nothing more than killing, robbing, and hurting, as well as the love of money, what else do you expect to see in the world but the same thing, and it seems that's all the world knows today? Even most of the games we find so many children and adults playing on the internet today are usually a lot more games of fighting, killing, or of some way of using the gun. But then we find so many people wondering why we see these kind of things going on so much in our world today. Now when I was growing up, there was a show that I just loved; yes, I loved it then, and I still love it today just as much, and it was called *The Andy Griffin Show*, and I just love it so much for just that reason, love. Yes, it's a show that's filled with love from beginning to end, and at the same time, it's very funny too, and it's considered to be a comedy show. Now comedy movies were always my favorite, for to me, it's better to laugh than cry. Now what turned me on so much about *The Andy Griffin Show* was again that as soon as it came on, from beginning to end, you saw love, love, and more love. First Andy and his family show nothing but love for each other, but on top of that, the whole town shows nothing else but love for each other, through the whole show, and again it's also just so funny. But my question is, why don't they still make TV programs like this for our children to look at today and get into? For I'm so sure that God wants us all to be just this way, yes, just filled and covered with love in every way. And what happened to Bugs Bunny and Daffy Duck? I mean, a lot of the cartoons they put on television today, I wouldn't even let my children look at. I mean, today they are showing cartoons that are showing different body parts, and they'd also be having cartoon characters using foul language. When I think my child is ready to learn about our different body parts, they'll learn in school or learn from me or their mother. Yes, I want my children to learn the right way, for I want me, my wife, and children to one day, after meeting

Jesus in the sky, hear Him tell us all, "Go through, my child." Again, death is a part of life for it's something we all shall experience, and that's why we don't go out of our minds when one does pass away, because for one, I must say one more time, death is another part of life, but right now, even more important than that is because it is a part of life and we all shall experience it, so we all should be trying to get ourselves right with God before it's too late and we can't, and for all those that take what I'm saying as foolishness, then you remember this. Here's something I remember my mother always saying that I know is so true, and it's if one's going down again, always remember, "*You can't cry over spilt milk.*" So, we must all begin to fix man's first and biggest mistake he ever made, which was when man stopped listening to God, and the only way we can fix this mistake is to once again begin listening to God in full. By getting ourselves right with God, and the only way you can be right with God is through Jesus Christ, His first Son, yes, Jesus Christ the saving Messiah, and believe me, there's only one Savior. You know, I once heard Trump say that Biden wasn't a savior, but Donald Trump isn't one either, for there's only one Savior: Jesus Christ. Now when Jesus Christ comes back to get what is His, and it all is very much His, He'll be coming back with the new heaven earth, and as God the Father first cast Satan, the devil, down from heaven when he went by the name of Lucifer, when he was an angel who was also called the Fourth Star but was cast down from heaven to the earth, yes, he's right on the earth with me and you at the moment, and that's why there's so much evil here on this earth. But when Christ comes back through those clouds, Satan will once again be cast down, only this time he will be cast all the way down into the lake of the fire of hell, and just as His Father did it, so will He, with a fist of fury. Besides Satan, out of all of God's creations, we've been His worse, for we're the only ones as Satan that ever turned our backs on God and let Him down when all He's done is love us and love us over and over again. For once again, we have a good God who gave His only begotten Son.

By** Jehovah* THROUGH THE HEART, MIND AND LEFT-HAND OF ***Kevin Moss

GOD'S BEEN A CLOUD OVER ME ALL MY LIFE WITH LOVE, LOVE, AND MORE LOVE

God the Father is Love, God the Son is Love, and God the
Holy Ghost is more Love. Love do we all want, and Love do we
all need, and true and real Love is what we get from He.
But the task is as we get it from Him; we must
learn to give it to all just like Him.
It doesn't matter what race, creed, or color one may
come to be, still to the other, Love must we.
For remember mine and your blood is red just like his, for truly
are we one, yes, every one of us human beings, so remember
one day you will die just like me! Yes, you will for the wage of
sin is death. Believe me, we all originate from Adam and Eve,
who put sin in us all, which brings on death wall to wall.
But if as Jesus Christ, you too put your hand out with Love to help
all with the same Love, when He does return, you too will He call.
Now I end saying once again we're so close to the end,
followed by the new beginning, my friends.
SO PLEASE, MAY WE ALL LEARN, LEARN, LEARN,
YES, LEARN HOW TO GIVE NOTHING ELSE
BUT LOVE, LOVE, AND MORE LOVE!

By Jehovah and Kevin Moss with Promising Love

A Stubborn People

"Now go, write it before them in a table, and note it in a book, that it may be for the times to come for ever and ever: That this is a rebellious people, lying children, children that will not hear the law of the Lord. Which say to the seers, see not; and to the prophets, Prophesy not unto us right things, speak unto us smooth things, prophesy deceits: Get you out of the way, turn aside out of the path, cause the Holy One of Israel to cease from before us. Wherefore thus saith the Holy One of Israel, because ye despise this word, and trust in oppression and perverseness, and stay thereon: therefore this iniquity shall be to you as a breach ready to fall, swelling out in a high wall, whose breaking cometh suddenly at an instant. And he shall break it as the breaking of the potters' vessel that is broken pieces; he shall not spare: so that there shall not be found in the bursting of it a sherd to take fire from the hearth, or to take water withal out of the pit. For thus saith the Lord God, the Holy One of Israel; In returning and rest shall you be saved; in quietness and in confidence shall be your strength; and ye would not, But ye said, No; for we will flee upon horses; therefore shall ye flee; and, We will ride upon the swift; therefore shall they that pursue you be swift. One thousand shall flee at the rebuke of one; at the rebuke of five shall ye flee; till ye be left as a beacon upon the top of a mountain, and as an ensign on a hill."

—ISAIAH 30:8–17

The Perilous Times Of The Last Days

"This second epistle, beloved, I now write unto you; in both which I stir up your pure minds by way of remembrance: That ye may be mindful of the words which were spoken before by the holy prophets, and of the commandment of the apostles of the Lord and Savior; Knowing this first, that there shall come in the last days scoffers, walking after their own lusts, And saying, where is the promise of His coming? For since the fathers fell asleep, all things continue as they were from the beginning of the creation. For this they willingly are ignorant of, that by the word of God the heavens were of old, and the earth standing out of the water and in the water: Whereby the world that then was, being overflowed with water, perished: But the heavens and the earth, which are now, by the same word are kept in store, reserved unto fire against the day of judgement and perdition of ungodly men. But beloved be not ignorant of this one thing, that one day is with the Lord as a thousand years, and a thousand years one day."

—2 PETER 3:1–8

The Greatest, The Greatest, The Greatest, God's Just The Greatest!

God's the greatest, the greatest, the greatest; yes, God's just the greatest!

Yes, He's the greatest there is, the greatest there ever was, and the greatest there ever will be.

Believe me, God is just the greatest; for instance, God once came down to speak with a servant of His.

Then the one who was with Him, yes, the Lord said to that servant:

> "And, they said unto him, where is Sarah thy wife? And he said be hold, in the tent.
>
> And he said, I will certainly return unto thee according to the time of life; and, lo, Sarah thy wife will have a son. And Sarah heard it in the tent door, which was behind him. Now Abraham and Sarah were old and well stricken in age; and it ceased to be with Sarah after manner of woman. Therefore Sarah laughed within herself, saying, After I'm waxed old shall I have pleasure, my lord being old also? And the Lord said unto Abraham, wherefore did Sarah laugh, saying, Shall I of a surety bear a child, which am old? Is anything too hard for the Lord? At the time appointed I will return unto thee."
>
> **—Genesis 18:10–14**

Now tell me, didn't Sarah have Isaac the following year? But how? Because God's just that great!

Now look at this.

Once there was a man named Joseph who was a son of Jacob and in the book of Genesis he was sold too Egypt by his own blood brothers!

"Come, and let us sell him to the Ish'-me-elites, and let not our hand be upon him; for he is our brother and our flesh. And his brethren were content."

—Genesis 37:27

Now when they got to Egypt Joseph was thrown in jail, but Joseph was determined to be faithful to the Lord and within a twinkle of an eye under God's command Joseph was Pharaoh's right hand man.

—Genesis 41:41

NOW TELL ME THAT WASN'T GREAT?
NOW IN THE BOOK OF 2 CHRONICLES 1:7.
"In that night did God appear unto Solomon and said unto him, "Ask what I shall give thee.""
And Solomon comes back with,
"Give me now wisdom and knowledge, that I may go out and come in before this people; for who can judge this thy people, that is so great?"

And God said to Solomon, "Because this was in thine heart, and thou has not asked riches, wealth, or honour, nor the life of thine enemies, neither yet has asked for long life; but has asked wisdom and knowledge for thy self, that thy may judge my people over whom I have made thee king: Wisdom and knowledge is granted unto thee; and I will thee riches and wealth, and honour."

NOW ISN'T *GOD* Just THE GREATEST?
(2 CHRONICLES 1:10-12)

www.ingramcontent.com/pod-product-compliance
Lightning Source LLC
LaVergne TN
LVHW091021080826
845145LV00002B/322

* 9 7 8 1 6 3 8 8 1 7 5 8 1 *